سيدنا آدم عليه السلام

The Father of Man

ADAM: LIFE & LEGACY

The Father of Man

ADAM

LIFE & LEGACY

KHALĪFAH OF QĀ'ID AL-MILLAH
Muftī Sayyid `Abdul Ṣamad al-Qādirī

TheSunniWay

ADAM: LIFE & LEGACY

contact@thesunniway.com

ISBN: 978-1-957773-38-4

DEDICATION

Dedicated to my link to 'Abū al-Bashar, upon him be salutations, and Sayyid al-Bashar, may Allāh send blessings and salutations upon him, my father, Sayyid 'Anwar Qādirī, the one who taught me to never compromise on the message of 'A`lā Ḥaḍrat, may Allāh have mercy upon him, and supported me throughout every hurdle along the way. *May Allāh Almighty protect him from all evils.*

FAQĪR SAYYID `ABDUL ṢAMAD AL-QĀDIRĪ
Khādim, TheSunniWay

CONTENTS

A NOTE FROM THE GRANDSON OF SADR AL-SHARI`AH

ALLĀH'S NAME TO BEGIN WITH, THE MOST COMPASSIONATE, THE EVER-MERCIFUL.
We praise Him, and we send blessings upon His Noble Messenger.

Upon seeing this book of Ḥaḍrat Mawlānā `Abdul Ṣamad Ṣāḥib, the eyes have lit up and the heart has become filled with joy. By writing a book concerning the biography and life story of our earliest father, 'Abū al-Bashar Sayyidunā 'Ādam, upon him be blessing and salutation, he has settled the debt which was over us *Sunnīs*. When making mention of Ḥaḍrat 'Ādam, upon him be blessing and salutation, people generally fall victim to exaggeration and negligence (*'ifrāṭ* and *tafrīṭ*), and they begin to narrate the story of the forbidden tree in the style and fashion of *'Isrā'īlīyāt*, even though he is the first human of this world and an honorable Prophet, and that to revere him is an obligation upon us. Allāh Almighty granted him the knowledge of everything in the world and made him the one prostrated to by the Angels, and due to disrespecting his court, He made 'Iblīs the accursed and the damned. Due to this, we should be very cautious in matters of his respect and honor. This book encompasses all of the necessary aspects of the life of Ḥaḍrat 'Ādam, upon him be blessing and salutation, and for many of our upcoming generations, it contains much to learn. The prayer is that Allāh Almighty accepts this effort of the author, and that He makes it beneficial for the people. *'Āmīn, by the honor of the Master of all Messengers, upon him, upon his progeny, and his companions be the most superior blessing and salutation.*

Faqīr [Muftī] Faizān al-Muṣṭafā Qādirī,
may he be pardoned

March 23, 2024
Ramaḍān al-Mubārak 12, 1445 H.

INTRODUCTION

الحمد لله رب العالمين ○ خالق الأرضين ○ الباعث فيها الأنبياء والمرسلين ○

والصلوة والسلام على من كان نبيا وآدم بين الماء والطين ○

Amongst the magnificent creations of Allāh Almighty, the first to be adorned in the garb of humanity was the *Ṣafī* (friend) of Allāh, Sayyidunā 'Ādam, upon him be salutations. He was the first human to be sent to Earth and the first of the approximate one hundred twenty-four thousand Prophets of Allāh, upon them be salutations, to be sent as guides for humankind.

Sayyidunā 'Ādam, upon him be salutations, being the first Prophet to step foot on Earth, was the first to bear the honor of preparing for the arrival of the one for whom the entire creation was brought into existence.

Allāh Almighty has granted Sayyidunā 'Ādam, upon him be salutations, the honor of being the father to all of mankind. Yet, when this father of man remembers the Final Messenger, may Allāh send blessings and salutations upon him, he says:

يا ابنى صورة وأبي معنى

O my son in appearance and my father in reality! [1]

[1] *Tajallī al-Yaqīn bi 'anna Nabīyyanā Sayyid al-Mursalīn*, pg. 40

This display of love and affection by Sayyidunā ʻĀdam, upon him be salutations, in the court of the Noble Prophet Muḥammad, may Allāh send blessings and salutations upon him, is testimony to the lofty rank Allāh Almighty has granted him as being the purpose of all creation and is in accordance with the message of the *Qur'ān*.

Allāh Almighty says:

مَا كَانَ مُحَمَّدٌ اَبَآ اَحَدٍ مِّنْ رِّجَالِكُمْ وَلٰكِنْ رَّسُوْلَ اللّٰهِ وَخَاتَمَ النَّبِيّٖنَ

Muḥammad is not the father of any of your men. However, he is the Messenger of Allāh and the Seal of all Prophets. [2]

In this verse of the Noble *Qur'ān*, Allāh Almighty informs that the Noble Messenger, may Allāh send blessings and salutations upon him, is not a father to any man – yet reminds that though he is not a biological father to any man, he is the Messenger of Allāh. This reminder following the negation of him being a biological father to any man emphasizes that though he is not a father to the men, his right to be honored and obeyed by his nation is much greater than that of a father.[3]

[2] *Sūrah al-'Aḥzāb: 40*

[3] *Khazā'in al-`Irfān, Sūrah al-'Aḥzāb: 40*

In this meaning, he is a father to all of creation as it is necessary for the creation to revere and manifest obedience in the court of the most beloved and most superior creation of Allāh, may Allāh send blessings and salutations upon him.

This is the reason for which Sayyidunā 'Ādam, upon him be salutations, while recognizing his own status of being a biological father to all of mankind, professes to the fact that Sayyidunā Rasūl Allāh, may Allāh send blessings and salutations upon him, is in a position far superior to a father for all of creation.

Sayyidunā 'Ādam, upon him be salutations, alongside being the first man to ever walk the face of the Earth, was the first man to bring the message of Allāh Almighty to those who would be birthed from his offspring.

His story is mentioned in great detail in the Noble *Qur'ān* and in the *Ḥadīth*, and this story of how man came to populate this planet is surely deserving of being studied.

The stories of those beloved to Allāh Almighty carry much wisdom and lessons for the people to learn from and be inspired by to walk in the footsteps of those who have undoubtedly succeeded in the purpose for which they are sent into the realm of existence. Such is also the case for the story of Sayyidunā 'Ādam, upon him be salutations.

I

INTRODUCING HUMANKIND

The story of Sayyidunā ʿĀdam, upon him be salutations, begins with Allāh Almighty sharing His intent for the creation of man amongst the infallible and innocent Angels.

Allāh Almighty mentions this occurrence in the Noble Qurʾān:

وَاِذْ قَالَ رَبُّكَ لِلْمَلَٰٓئِكَةِ اِنِّيْ جَاعِلٌ فِي الْاَرْضِ خَلِيْفَةً ۖ قَالُوْٓا اَتَجْعَلُ فِيْهَا مَنْ يُّفْسِدُ فِيْهَا
وَيَسْفِكُ الدِّمَآءَ ۚ وَنَحْنُ نُسَبِّحُ بِحَمْدِكَ وَنُقَدِّسُ لَكَ ۖ قَالَ اِنِّيْٓ اَعْلَمُ مَا لَا تَعْلَمُوْنَ

And [remember!] when your Lord said to the Angels, "I will be creating,
in the land, a vice-regent." They said, "Will you make in it one who causes
corruption therein and sheds blood while we glorify You by Your praise
and proclaim Your sanctity?" He said, "Indeed, I know what you do not
know." [4]

---

[4] *Sūrah al-Baqarah: 30*

In this verse, it is seen that Allāh Almighty informs the *Malā'ikah* of His intent to create a *khalīfah* in the land, an individual of authority who will enforce the laws and commands of the Creator Almighty. Moreover, although every Prophet is a *khalīfah* of Allāh Almighty, this verse particularly speaks of Sayyidunā 'Ādam, upon him be salutations.[5]

Allāh Almighty appointing a *khalīfah* for the people of the land is a manifestation of His all-encompassing mercy and favor upon His creation. Despite having no need for someone to represent Him in the lands, Allāh Almighty has established this system of representatives, beginning with Sayyidunā 'Ādam, upon him be salutations, and concluding with Sayyidunā Muḥammad Rasūl Allāh, may Allāh send blessings and salutations upon him. Those reaping the benefits of this system are the ones dwelling within the world.

One of the many wisdoms of the appointment of a *khalīfah* is that the creation severely lacks in the ability to acquire blessings from the pure court of Allāh Almighty and to do so without a medium is not within the capacity of an ordinary human. The One who grants these blessings is pure and sanctified while those who seek these blessings are surrounded and captured by the affairs and negativities of the world.[6]

[5] *Khazā'in al-`Irfān, Sūrah al-Baqarah: 30*

[6] *Tafsīr Rūḥ al-Bayān, Sūrah al-Baqarah: 30*

The appointment of a *khalīfah* gives man a medium by the means of whom they reap the blessings of Allāh Almighty and present themselves in His sanctified court.

Prior to this point in time, it was a group of the *Malā'ikah* who inhabited the Earth and acted as the representatives of Allāh Almighty on land, and, at this point, they were being conveyed the news of their replacement by a *khalīfah* superior to them.[7]

Originally, when Allāh Almighty created the land and the skies, He also created the *Malā'ikah* and the *Jinn*. The *Malā'ikah* were made to inhabit the skies while the *Jinn* populated the Earth.

The father of *Jinn*-kind was named Jānn and he was created from a smokeless flame of fire. He was commanded to live on land and from his offspring, the population of the *Jinn*-kind grew. The *Jinn*-kind populated the Earth for an extensive period of time. When the evils of jealousy and rebellion began to sow their seeds within their communities, they became corrupt and began killing one another.

In order to combat this corruption which had soiled the communities of the *Jinn*, Allāh Almighty had sent an army of the *Malā'ikah* onto the Earth.

[7] *ibid*

This battalion of the *Malā'ikah* was sent in the leadership of 'Iblīs, who, at the time, manifested superiority in knowledge in comparison to the *Malā'ikah* and thus led the Angels in this battle against evil.

In a matter of no time following their descent to land, the *Malā'ikah* defeated the *Jinn* and banished them to islands[8] and caves of mountains far away from their previously occupied habitats.

Upon this victory, the *Malā'ikah* who had come to the Earth began to live there themselves and as a result, their burden of worship was lightened.

In return for the role played by 'Iblīs in the reformation of the land, he was granted the rulership of the land and the sky alongside being bestowed the treasure of Paradise.

He would worship Allāh Almighty at times on land, at times in the sky, and sometimes, he would worship Allāh Almighty in Paradise.

As a result of this honor bestowed upon him and the freedom he was given to travel throughout the land, the skies, and Paradise, a sense of self-admiration stemmed from him. He thought to himself, "Allāh has granted me this rulership because no one amongst the Angels is more honorable than me."[9]

[8] *Tafsīr al-Khāzin, Sūrah al-Baqarah: 30*

[9] *Tafsīr Rūḥ al-Bayān, Sūrah al-Baqarah: 30*

It was this same arrogance and self-admiration that can be seen embedding its roots here which would lead to his eventual destruction and his perpetual and ever-lasting torment in the scorching flames of hell.

One view of the *mufassirūn* states that it was these *Malā'ikah*, those in the army of 'Iblīs inhabiting the Earth, who were being addressed by this news of Allāh Almighty creating a *khalīfah* in the land.[10]

The word *khalīfah* also denotes a successor or someone who would come after another. This news alerted these *Malā'ikah* that their task of representing Allāh Almighty in the lands had come to an end and they were now to be replaced by a human.[11]

It was possibly due to these priorly witnessed series of events, and the corruption caused by the *Jinn* on land that the *Malā'ikah* reacted to this news in a manner that exhibits perplexity.

However, the intent of the *Malā'ikah* was not to object to the divine will of Allāh Almighty and nor to criticize Sayyidunā 'Ādam, upon him be salutations. Their intent was to learn of Allāh's wisdom in appointing a *khalīfah*.[12]

[10] *ibid*

[11] *ibid*

[12] *Khazā'in al-`Irfān, Sūrah al-Baqarah: 30*

Furthermore, in their question, their knowledge of the corruptions that would surround humankind is manifested. This knowledge of theirs was either given to them directly by Allāh Almighty, was something they had seen in the *Lawḥ Maḥfūẓ* (Sacred Tablet), or was a result of their judgement according to previous experiences with the *Jinn*.[13]

The fact of the *Malā'ikah* being allowed the opportunity to speak their opinion in this regard is surely an exhibition of Allāh's unconstrained wisdom. He Almighty who possesses limitless knowledge has no need to consult even a single soul for His decisions, yet He honors His creation with what seems like a consultation with these Angels.

There are many wisdoms in this consultation and one of these divine wisdoms is a lesson for the creation: seeking advice in your affairs from those who are worthy of trust is an act beloved to Allāh Almighty.

Moreover, it is possible that Allāh Almighty wanted the *Malā'ikah* to ask the question that they did in order to bring to light the status and lofty rank of Sayyidunā 'Ādam, upon him be salutations, before them.

He is yet to be created and has already been bestowed the crown of being Allāh's *khalīfah*.[14]

[13] *ibid*

[14] *Tafsīr Rūḥ al-Bayān, Sūrah al-Baqarah: 30*

Furthermore, it is said that the slave sincere to the master does not prefer that another slave be brought into service who would disobey the master. Thus, knowing what would stem from the offspring of Sayyidunā 'Ādam, upon him be salutations, the Angels asked this question in their love and reverence for the majestic court of Allāh Almighty.[15]

The *Malā'ikah* spend their time solely in the worship of Allāh Almighty, and even the idea of disobeying Allāh Almighty does not cross their pure thoughts.

However, despite this, Allāh Almighty informs the *Malā'ikah* that they cannot completely perceive the wisdom behind the divine decisions of Allāh Almighty and that He knows what they do not.

In other words, He tells them that His wisdom is beyond their comprehension and that within the creation of humankind exist profound wisdoms.

Although there will be corruption and evils amongst the humankind, it is this very creation amongst whom Allāh Almighty will send those most beloved to Him from His Prophets, upon them be salutations, the scholars, and the *'Awliyā'*.[16]

[15] *Tafsīr al-Khāzin, Sūrah al-Baqarah: 30*

[16] *Khazā'in al-`Irfān, Sūrah al-Baqarah: 30*

2

THE CREATION OF MANKIND'S FATHER

Sayyidunā Wahb bin Munabbih, Allāh is pleased with him, narrates that when Allāh Almighty intended to bring Sayyidunā 'Ādam, upon him be salutations, to the realm of existence, He said to the Earth, "Indeed, I will create from you such a creation from amongst whom some will obey Me, and some will disobey Me. Thus, whomsoever of them obeys Me, I will admit them into *Jannah* and whomsoever of them disobeys Me, I will admit them into the fire."

The Earth responded, "Will You create from me such a creation that will be for the fire?"

Allāh Almighty responded, "Yes."

Thus, the Earth broke down into tears and springs erupted which would flow to the Day of *Qiyāmah*.

In one account of this occurrence, the Earth complained, "O Allāh, I will become deficient by the taking of soil!"

Allāh Almighty responded, "Do not fear. When it returns to you, it will be even more beautiful and fragrant than before."

This is one of the wisdoms behind applying fragrance to those who pass away before being returned to the possession of the Earth.[17]

Thereafter, Allāh Almighty sent Sayyidunā Jibrīl, upon him be salutations, to the Earth to bring a handful of the red, black, pure, and bad parts of the Earth. When Sayyidunā Jibrīl, upon him be salutations, approached the Earth, it pleaded, "I seek refuge in the honor of Allāh, the One who sent you to me, from you taking anything away from me!"

`Allāmah 'Ismā`īl Ḥaqqī, may Allāh have mercy upon him, mentions that the wisdom behind taking different types and colors of the soil for the creation of Sayyidunā 'Ādam, upon him be salutations, is that the children of Sayyidunā 'Ādam, upon him be salutations, themselves come in different colors and bear various differing characteristics.[18]

[17] *Tafsīr Rūḥ al-Bayān, Sūrah al-Baqarah: 30*

[18] *ibid*

Upon this reaction from the Earth, Sayyidunā Jibrīl, upon him be salutations, returned to his station and said, "O my Lord, it sought Your refuge from me, so I did not prefer that I proceed towards it."

Then, Allāh Almighty commanded Sayyidunā Mīkā'īl, upon him be salutations, "Go and bring Me a handful of it." When he approached the Earth to take from it, the Earth said to him the same as it had said to Sayyidunā Jibrīl, upon him be salutations.

He too returned to his station and reported to Allāh Almighty what the Earth had said.

After this, Allāh Almighty said to Sayyidunā `Izrā'īl, upon him be salutations, "Go and bring Me a handful from the Earth."

When he approached the Earth, the Earth said, "I seek refuge in the honor of Allāh, the One who sent you, from you taking anything from me!"

He responded, "And I seek refuge in His honor from disobeying Him in any matter."

Then, he took a handful from each of its regions, some from that which was pleasant, some from the saline, the sweet, the bitter, the pure, and the bad.

Every speck of that soil would become the bodies of all humans and from whichever location the speck of dirt of any human is taken, that is precisely where he is returned upon his burial.[19]

He ascended with it to the sky and Allāh Almighty questioned him despite already knowing what had occurred.

Sayyidunā `Izrā'īl, upon him be salutations, reported what the Earth had said to him and how he responded to the Earth's cry for sympathy.

Allāh Almighty responded, "By My honor and My majesty, I will most definitely create a creation from that which you have brought, and I will surely commission you upon the seizing of their souls due to the lack of your sympathy!"[20]

Due to Sayyidunā `Izrā'īl, upon him be salutations, successfully carrying out this task without paying heed to the Earth's cries for sympathy, he was appointed as the Angel who would seize the souls of humankind, and even today, no matter how much man cries for an extension on life, pleads for mercy, or tries to flee from the grasp of death, Sayyidunā `Izrā'īl, upon him be salutations, the Angel of Death, takes their soul on the command of Allāh Almighty.

[19] *ibid*

[20] *Tafsīr al-Khāzin, Sūrah al-Baqarah: 30*

Thereafter, Allāh Almighty placed half of that handful in *Jannah* and the other half in the hellfire. Then, He left it there for as long as He Almighty willed.[21]

In another account of this incident, Sayyidunā `Izrā'īl, upon him be salutations, was commanded to put half into the hellfire and half in *Jannah*, and then to place it in *Wādī Nu`mān* which is situated in the middle of *Makkah Mukarramah* and *Ṭā'if.*[22]

Thereafter, it was taken out of there and the structure of Sayyidunā 'Ādam, upon him be salutations, was prepared.

One narration shows that in the time that Allāh Almighty had left the soil to be used in the sculpting of Sayyidunā 'Ādam, upon him be salutations, it was showered by a cloud of sorrow for thirty-nine years. Afterwards, for only one year, it was showered by a rain of peace and tranquility.

This is the reason for which the children of 'Ādam, upon him be salutations, are surrounded by grief and sorrow but they ultimately achieve solace.[23]

There is a difference of opinion amongst the scholars as to where exactly Sayyidunā 'Ādam, upon him be salutations, was brought to life.

[21] *ibid*

[22] *Tafsīr Rūḥ al-Bayān, Sūrah al-Baqarah: 30*

[23] *ibid*

Some say that this took place in the sky of Earth, some say it was in a garden on Earth which is a respected location, and others say he was born in *Jannah `Adn* and was removed from it thereafter.[24]

The prophetic narrations also inform of the day in which Sayyidunā ʿĀdam, upon him be salutations, was created.

Sayyidunā ʿAbū Hurayrah, Allāh is pleased with him, states:

أخذ رسول الله صلى الله عليه وسلم بيدى فقال خلق الله عزوجل التربة يوم السبت

وخلق فيها الجبال يوم الأحد وخلق الشجر يوم الإثنين وخلق المكروه يوم الثلاثاء

وخلق النور يوم الأربعاء وبث فيها الدواب يوم الخميس وخلق آدم عليه السلام بعد

العصر من يوم الجمعة فى آخر الخلق وفى آخر ساعة من ساعات الجمعة

فيما بين العصر إلى الليل

The Messenger of Allāh, may Allāh send blessings and salutations upon him, took my hand and said, "Allāh, the Sublime and the Majestic, created the soil on Saturday. He created the mountains in it on Sunday. He created the tree on Monday. He created that which entails labor on Tuesday. He created the light on Wednesday. He spread the animals throughout it on Thursday. He created ʿĀdam, upon him be salutations, after `Aṣr on Friday in the end of the creation, in the last hour amongst the hours of Friday in what is between `Aṣr and the night." [25]

This narration shows that Sayyidunā ʿĀdam, upon him be salutations, was created on the best of all days – a Friday.

[24] *ibid*

[25] *Ṣaḥīḥ Muslim: 2789*

Upon reading this narration, the question could arise that how is it possible that Sayyidunā 'Ādam, upon him be salutations, was created after a long period of time after the *Jinn* inhabited the Earth while this narration shows that he was born on Friday and the Earth was created on Saturday?

The response to this confusion is that this narration does not specify that the Friday in which Sayyidunā 'Ādam, upon him be salutations, was created was the Friday which immediately followed the Saturday in which the Earth was created.

It is possible that this Friday in which Sayyidunā 'Ādam, upon him be salutations, was created was after an extended period of time.[26]

When the bodily structure of Sayyidunā 'Ādam, upon him be salutations, had been prepared, it was left on the door of *Jannah* and the *Malā'ikah* would look at the blessed body in awe due to never having seen anything like it.[27]

This magnificent physical form of Sayyidunā 'Ādam, upon him be salutations, by which the noble and infallible *Malā'ikah* were struck with astonishment and filled with admiration is described in several prophetic narrations.

[26] *Tafsīr al-Maẓharī, Sūrah al-Baqarah: 30*

[27] *Tafsīr al-Khāzin, Sūrah al-Baqarah: 30*

A narration recorded by 'Imām Bukhārī, may Allāh have mercy upon him, states that the most beloved and superior-most Prophet of Allāh, the Purpose of Creation, Sayyidunā Rasūl Allāh, may Allāh send blessings and salutations upon him, says:

خلق الله آدم وطوله ستون ذراعا ثم قال اذهب فسلم على أولئك من الملائكة فاستمع ما
يحيونك تحيتك وتحية ذريتك فقال السلام عليكم فقالوا السلام عليك ورحمة الله
فزادوه ورحمة الله فكل من يدخل الجنة على صورة آدم فلم يزل الخلق ينقص حتى الآن

Allāh created 'Ādam and his height was sixty cubits. Then, He said, "Go and greet those of the Malā'ikah and listen closely to how they respond to you for it is your greeting and the greeting of your offspring." Thus, he said, "al-Salām `alaykum." They responded, "al-Salām `alayka wa raḥmat-Allāh." Thus, they added, "Wa raḥmat-Allāh." So, everyone who will enter Paradise will be upon the appearance of 'Ādam and the creation has continuously decreased [in stature] up until now. [28]

In this narration, the breath-taking height of Sayyidunā 'Ādam, upon him be salutations, is mentioned; he was sixty cubits tall. This was the original build and structure of humankind, but this narration mentions that the humans continuously, era after era, decreased in height and stature and ultimately reached the height and stature that the humans are commonly seen in today.

[28] *Ṣaḥīḥ al-Bukhārī: 3326*

Moreover, in another narration of Sayyidunā 'Abū Hurayrah, Allāh is pleased with him, there is mention of his height and his width, detailing even further this magnificent and awe-striking build:

كان طول آدم ستين ذراعا في سبعة أذرع عرضا

The height of 'Ādam was sixty cubits in seven cubits of breadth. [29]

The unit of measurement used to describe the height and width of mankind's father, Sayyidunā 'Ādam, upon him be salutations, in these narrations is a cubit or a *dhirā`*.

This is a unit of measurement which denotes the length from one's elbow to the tip of the middle finger.

In a portion of another narration describing the marvelous build of Sayyidunā 'Ādam, upon him be salutations, Sayyidunā `Aṭā' bin 'Abū Rabāḥ, Allāh is pleased with him, states:

لما خلق الله آدم في الجنة كان رجلاه في الأرض ورأسه في السماء يسمع كلام أهل السماء ودعاءهم ويأنس إليهم

When Allāh created 'Ādam in Paradise, his feet were on land while his head was in the sky. He would hear the talks of those residing in the sky and their supplications, and he would observe them. [30]

[29] *`Umdah al-Qārī: Ḥadīth 3326*
[30] *ibid*

This was the build of Sayyidunā 'Ādam, upon him be salutations, when Allāh Almighty had created him.

In another narration further detailing the admirable appearance of Sayyidunā 'Ādam, upon him be salutations, Sayyidunā 'Ubay bin Ka`b, Allāh is pleased with him, says:

إن الله تعالى خلق آدم رجلا طوالا كثير شعر الرأس كأنه نخلة سحوق

Indeed, Allāh created 'Ādam as a tall man, one abundant in the hair of the head as if he was a vast palm tree. [31]

These narrations give some insight as to why it was that the *Malā'ikah* would gaze at the blessed structure and build of Sayyidunā 'Ādam, upon him be salutations, in a state of awe and astonishment. Allāh Almighty had created him unlike any other creation witnessed by the Angels prior to him.

As the physical structure of Sayyidunā 'Ādam, upon him be salutations, laid at the gates of *Jannah* and the Angels would admire his magnificence, the roots of jealousy strengthened their grip on the intellect of 'Iblīs and the dark clouds of arrogance began to take their place as a barrier to his conscience.

Just as the *Malā'ikah* would pass by the blessed body of Sayyidunā 'Ādam, upon him be salutations, a day came wherein 'Iblīs would witness this magnificent creation of Allāh Almighty resting at the gates of *Jannah*.

[31] *ibid*

He saw the blessed body and said, "Why has he been created?"

He struck his hand on his body and found it to be fragile and delicate. His hand went through the blessed body and came out from the other side. He then said to the *Malā'ikah* in his company, "He has been created fragile and thus, he will not be able to remain firm in anything. Now tell me – if he is made superior to you, what will you do?"

They responded, "We will obey the command of our Master."

The accursed 'Iblīs thought to himself, "If he is made superior to me, I will not remain obedient to him. If he is given under my rule, I will humiliate him."

Thereafter, he gathered his saliva and placed it in the area of Sayyidunā 'Ādam's navel. Allāh Almighty commanded Sayyidunā Jibrīl, upon him be salutations, to scrape the saliva away from the navel.

According to `Allāmah 'Ismā`īl Ḥaqqī, may Allāh have mercy upon him, the depth of the navel found in humankind is due to Sayyidunā Jibrīl, upon him be salutations, scraping away the soil from the area of the navel and from this soil that was scraped away, the dog was created.

This is the reason for which three characteristics are found in dogs:

1. They grow close to humans because they were created from the soil of Sayyidunā 'Ādam, upon him be salutations.
2. They spend the nights awake because their soil was touched by Sayyidunā Jibrīl, upon him be salutations.
3. At times, they go rabid and attack humans due to the impact of 'Iblīs' saliva.[32]

Eventually, Allāh Almighty had intended to bring this structure to life by allowing the soul to take its place in his body. When Allāh Almighty intended to inspirit this first form of man, He commanded the soul to enter the body of Sayyidunā 'Ādam, upon him be salutations.

When the soul looked, it saw a narrow entrance into the body and said, "O my Lord, how shall I enter this body?"

Allāh Almighty said to it, "Enter it forcibly and soon you shall be removed from it forcibly."[33]

In another account of this occurrence, when Allāh Almighty commanded the soul to enter, the soul pleaded, "My Lord, this place is very deep, and this place is extremely dark."

[32] *Tafsīr Rūḥ al-Bayān, Sūrah al-Baqarah: 30*

[33] *Tafsīr al-Khāzin, Sūrah al-Baqarah: 30*

The soul was commanded to enter a second and third time, yet both times, it presented excuses and afterwards, it entered on its own.

Allāh Almighty said, "You enter forcibly so you shall find great difficulty in exiting."

This is the reason that man faces a great amount of pain and distress at the time in which the soul leaves his body.[34]

According to some narrations, when the soul was reluctant to enter even after being commanded several times, the structure was enlightened by the light of Sayyidunā Rasūl Allāh, may Allāh send blessings and salutations upon him.

That light was entrusted to Sayyidunā 'Ādam, upon him be salutations, and kept in his forehead. It was only after this that the soul found the courage within itself to enter the body of Sayyidunā 'Ādam, upon him be salutations, and slowly began to enter.[35]

The soul took its entrance from the vertex of the head, reached the eyes, and he began to look at the rest of his body in the form of clay. Then, the soul reached his nostrils and he sneezed. When the soul approached his tongue, he said, "*al-Ḥamdu li Allāh Rabb al-`Ālamīn* (All praise be to Allāh, the Lord of all Creations)."

[34] *Tafsīr Rūḥ al-Bayān, Sūrah al-Baqarah: 30*

[35] *Tafsīr Na`īmī, Sūrah al-Baqarah: 30*

These were his first words to which Allāh Almighty responded:

رحمك ربك يا أبا محمد ولهذا خلقتك

May your Lord show you mercy O 'Abū Muḥammad!
This is what I have created you for.

When the soul reached the knees, he attempted to stand but was unable to do so and Allāh Almighty said:

خُلِقَ الْإِنْسَانُ مِنْ عَجَلٍ

Man was created of haste. [36]

When the soul reached the shins and feet, he stood up as a complete composite of man – made up of flesh, blood, bones, veins, nerves, and all that is found in the body of a human; he had come to life. He was clothed in attire made from nail which increased his body in beauty day after day.[37]

This magnificent creation of Allāh Almighty by whose witnessing the *Malā'ikah* were already in a state of astonishment had come to life and this was only the beginning of their witnessing the wonders of Sayyidunā 'Ādam, upon him be salutations, and that of his offspring.

[36] *Sūrah al-'Anbiyā': 37*

[37] *Tafsīr al-Khāzin, Sūrah al-Baqarah: 30*

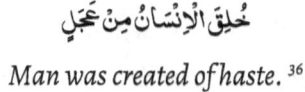

3

SUPERIORITY BY KNOWLEDGE

After the first form of man had been brought to life, Allāh Almighty intended to manifest the superiority of His creation above all the *Malā'ikah* who stood watching in awe.

This incident is mentioned in the Noble *Qur'ān* as Allāh Almighty states:

وَعَلَّمَ اٰدَمَ الْاَسْمَآءَ كُلَّهَا ثُمَّ عَرَضَهُمْ عَلَى الْمَلٰٓئِكَةِ فَقَالَ اَنْۢبِـُٔوْنِيْ بِاَسْمَآءِ هٰٓؤُلَآءِ اِنْ كُنْتُمْ صٰدِقِيْنَ ۞ قَالُوْا سُبْحٰنَكَ لَا عِلْمَ لَنَآ اِلَّا مَا عَلَّمْتَنَا اِنَّكَ اَنْتَ الْعَلِيْمُ الْحَكِيْمُ ۞ قَالَ يٰٓاٰدَمُ اَنْۢبِئْهُمْ بِاَسْمَآئِهِمْ فَلَمَّآ اَنْۢبَاَهُمْ بِاَسْمَآئِهِمْ قَالَ اَلَمْ اَقُلْ لَّكُمْ اِنِّيْٓ اَعْلَمُ غَيْبَ السَّمٰوٰتِ وَالْاَرْضِ وَاَعْلَمُ مَا تُبْدُوْنَ وَمَا كُنْتُمْ تَكْتُمُوْنَ ۞

And He taught 'Ādam the names of all things, then presented them all to the Angels and said, "Tell Me the names of these if you are truthful." They said, "Glory to You! We have no knowledge except of that which You have taught us. Indeed, You are the All-Knowing and All-Wise."

He said, "O 'Ādam, inform them the names of them all." So, when he informed them of all of their names, He said, "Did I not tell you that I know all of the things hidden in the skies and land, and I know all that you manifest and all that you conceal?" [38]

It is witnessed in these verses that when Allāh Almighty intended to demonstrate the superiority of man, He manifested this superiority of the Noble Sayyidunā 'Ādam, upon him be salutations, through the unmatched knowledge that was granted to him. Despite the many ways by which his superiority could be manifested, Allāh Almighty chose to do so by means of knowledge.

When Sayyidunā 'Ādam, upon him be salutations, was created, the infallible *Malā'ikah* said, "Our Lord will create whatever He has willed, but will never create a creation superior to us in knowledge. And even if he is, we are more knowing than him because we were created before him, and we have experienced what he has never seen."[39]

This assumption which had made its way to the innocent thoughts of the infallible *Malā'ikah* was soon put to rest when Allāh Almighty asked of them to demonstrate the same caliber of knowledge manifested by Sayyidunā 'Ādam, upon him be salutations.

[38] *Sūrah al-Baqarah: 31-33*

[39] *Tafsīr al-Khāzin, Sūrah al-Baqarah: 31*

The very field in which the *Malā'ikah* had not expected to be surpassed in is the one in which Allāh Almighty had manifested his superiority and lofty rank to leave no doubt in his superiority above them all.

The purpose of this entire occurrence was to establish the superiority of Sayyidunā 'Ādam, upon him be salutations, and to manifest His wisdom in creating man. Allāh Almighty did not do so except by demonstrating the unparalleled knowledge of this creation of His.

Had there been any quality more eminent than knowledge, Allāh Almighty would certainly have established his superiority by that, and not by knowledge.[40]

This entire occurrence is testimony to the virtue of knowledge and its importance. The virtue of the religion's knowledge is a concept emphasized time and time again in the Holy *Qur'ān* and the *Ḥadīth*, yet the people fail to understand its importance. In order to understand the way by which Allāh Almighty manifested the superiority of Sayyidunā 'Ādam, upon him be salutations, one must understand the eminence of knowledge.

Knowledge is a quality which the rationale willingly accepts as a praiseworthy trait. If an individual is a scholar and is blamed of ignorance, he will be hurt by this blame despite recognizing the dishonesty within the claim.

[40] *Tafsīr Kabīr, Sūrah al-Baqarah: 31*

On the other side of the coin, if a man of ignorance is mistakenly called a scholar or a person of knowledge, he will feel delighted by such a claim despite knowing that it is a lie.[41]

This speaks to the fact that the natural disposition of man has accepted knowledge to be a praiseworthy quality and holds it in high regard. The Messenger of Allāh, may Allāh send blessings and salutations upon him, he who bears the secrets of the unseen in his pure chest, has also emphasized the importance and virtue of knowledge.

Regarding those who were granted this treasure of knowledge, the Beloved Messenger, may Allāh send blessings and salutations upon him, states:

من صلى خلف عالم من العلماء فكأنما صلى خلف نبي من الأنبياء

He who prays behind any scholar from amongst the scholars, it is as if he has prayed behind a Prophet from amongst the Prophets. [42]

The men of knowledge deliver the people to the path beloved to Allāh Almighty and become a means of guidance due to this knowledge. The result of this sacred knowledge is superior to all of the treasures the world possesses.

[41] *ibid*

[42] *ibid*

When sending the Door to the City of Knowledge, Sayyidunā `Alī al-Murtaḍā, Allāh is pleased with him, to Yemen, the Noble Messenger, may Allāh send blessings and salutations upon him, said:

لأن يهدى الله بك رجلا واحدا خير لك مما تطلع عليه الشمس أو تغرب

That Allāh guides one man through you is better for you than all that the sun rises or sets on. [43]

If this is the result of bringing one individual to the path of guidance, what can be imagined of the reward for those who spend their days and nights calling the people to the path of the pious? This is the blessing and virtue of those who possess this bounty of knowledge in their lifetimes. However, their status even upon their passing has been exhibited by the Beloved Prophet, may Allāh send blessings and salutations upon him.

The Noble Messenger, may Allāh send blessings and salutations upon him, states:

معلم الخير إذا مات بكى عليه طير السماء ودواب الأرض وحيتان البحور

The teacher of good, when he dies, the birds of the sky, the animals of the land, and the fish of the seas cry for him. [44]

This lofty status granted to the scholars of the religion is a blessing of the knowledge they carry in their hearts.

[43] *ibid*

[44] *ibid*

Regarding this virtue, Sayyidunā `Alī al-Murtaḍā, Allāh is pleased with him, states, "The knowledge of the religion is superior to wealth for seven reasons:

1) Knowledge is the inheritance of the Prophets whereas wealth is the inheritance of Fir`awn, Hāmān, Shaddād, and Namrūd.
2) Upon being spent, wealth is decreased whereas knowledge is increased.
3) Man protects wealth whereas knowledge safeguards man.
4) Following death, wealth remains in the world whereas knowledge accompanies one to the grave.
5) Wealth is given to both believers and disbelievers alike whereas the benefit of religious knowledge is only acquired by the faithful.
6) No one can be independent of a scholar, whereas many people have no need for the wealthy.
7) Through knowledge, one attains steadiness upon the Bridge of *Ṣirāṭ*, and from wealth, instability.[45]

This statement of Sayyidunā `Alī, Allāh is pleased with him, is surely a great reminder for those who live in a time wherein the people surround their hearts and minds with the love of wealth and view the scholars of the religion as inferior. The wealth that makes one superior is not worldly riches – it is the knowledge of the religion.

[45] *Tafsīr Na`īmī, Sūrah al-Baqarah: 31*

This is the status of this virtue of knowledge that Allāh Almighty has bestowed unto man. This is what sets man apart from beast. Man is not superior to animal due to his strength, or due to his ability to feed himself and provide. Had strength been the scale of judgment for superiority, then there are many animals against whose strength man does not stand a chance. Had the basis of judgment been the ability to provide and eat, then man is seen struggling day and night for the sake of provision and is left unhappy at the end of the blood, sweat, and tears he sheds for a living, whereas an animal hunts for a few hours in a day and finds contentment within its earnings. It is only knowledge which brings man to a position superior to beast.

Knowledge is such a blessing that even if acquired by a dog, its hunt becomes permissible for consumption. If a dog untrained for hunting successfully kills its hunt, that hunt cannot be consumed. But, if the same dog is trained for the sake of hunting, the animal it kills can be consumed. This is the blessing of knowledge.[46]

It is this treasure of knowledge that can even give something as seemingly insignificant as an ant a status which others would gaze at with eyes of astonishment.

[46] *ibid*

Due to knowledge, the ant of Sayyidunā Sulaymān, upon him be salutations, was given such a status that not only was it granted the honor of mention in the Noble *Qur'ān*, but there is also an entire chapter named after it, *Sūrah al-Naml*, The Chapter of the Ant.

Moreover, Allāh Almighty was so pleased by its words, He recorded its words within the Noble *Qur'ān*.[47]

It is knowledge that distinguishes man from beast and gives even an animal a rank above its like.

But what was the degree of this knowledge granted to Sayyidunā 'Ādam, upon him be salutations, which would deem him worthy of being prostrated to out of honor and reverence by the infallible *Malā'ikah*?

Whereas the aforementioned verse of the Glorious *Qur'ān* mentions that Sayyidunā 'Ādam, upon him be salutations, was granted the knowledge of all names, the *mufassirūn* give insight as to what exactly it was from the treasures of knowledge that was bestowed unto Sayyidunā 'Ādam, upon him be salutations, and as to what exactly is this knowledge of names.

[47] *ibid*

In this regard, the position of Sayyidunā `Abd Allāh 'ibn `Abbās, Allāh is pleased with them, is recorded by the noble exegetes of the *Qur'ān* and his position regarding the exegesis of the Noble *Qur'ān* is surely one of authority as he himself narrates:

ضمني رسول الله صلى الله عليه وسلم وقال اللهم علمه الكتاب

The Messenger of Allāh, may Allāh send blessings and salutations upon him, embraced me and said, "O Allāh, grant him knowledge of the Book."[48]

Sayyidunā `Abd Allāh 'ibn `Abbās, Allāh is pleased with them, the one who has been granted the knowledge of the Divine Book of Allāh Almighty by the blessed supplication of the Noble Messenger, may Allāh send blessings and salutations upon him, states:

علمه اسم كل شيء حتى القصعة والقصيعة

He taught him the name of every single thing,
even of the big and small bowl.[49]

Sayyidunā `Abd Allāh 'ibn `Abbās, Allāh is pleased with them, explicitly mentions that the name of everything was taught to Sayyidunā 'Ādam, upon him be salutations, even something so insignificant as a bowl; he was even taught the different names for the small and big bowls.

[48] *Ṣaḥīḥ al-Bukhārī: 75*

[49] *Tafsīr al-Khāzin, Sūrah al-Baqarah: 31*

Tafsīr Maẓharī, referencing *Baghawī*, attributes this exact position to 'Imām Mujāhid and 'Imām Qatādah alongside being that of Sayyidunā `Abd Allāh 'ibn `Abbās, Allāh is pleased with them.[50]

This position is further clarified in the statement attributed to Sayyidunā `Abd Allāh 'ibn `Abbās, Allāh is pleased with them, `Ikramah, Mujāhid, and 'Ibn Jubayr:

علمه أسماء جميع الأشياء كلها جليلها وحقيرها

He taught him the names of everything, all of them – the significant and the insignificant of them. [51]

According to this position, Sayyidunā 'Ādam, upon him be salutations, was granted the knowledge of the names for all things in existence, to the extent that he was even taught the names of the various forms of technology that are found in this day which were unimagined and unfathomed even a few centuries prior.

Besides this position of Sayyidunā `Abd Allāh 'ibn `Abbās, Allāh is pleased with them, various other statements of the *mufassirūn* are seen in this regard which detail this vast ocean of knowledge that was bestowed unto Sayyidunā 'Ādam, upon him be salutations.

[50] *Tafsīr al-Maẓharī, Sūrah al-Baqarah: 31*

[51] *Tafsīr al-Qurṭubī, Sūrah al-Baqarah: 31*

The method of this teaching, alongside detail of that which was taught, is also mentioned:

خلق الله كل شيء من الحيوان والجماد وغير ذلك وعلم آدم أسماءها كلها فقال يا آدم هذا بعير وهذا فرس وهذه شاة حتى أتى على آخرها

Allāh created everything from the animate and inanimate objects, and things other than those, and taught 'Ādam their names, all of them. Thereupon, He said, "O 'Ādam, this is a camel, this is a horse, this is a goat," up until He reached the last of them. [52]

This position clarifies that Sayyidunā 'Ādam, upon him be salutations, was not only taught the names of said things without any recognition of what those names were used for, rather he was shown each and every one of the things for which he learned a name.

Supporting this very position is a statement of 'Imām Qatādah, may Allāh have mercy upon him, regarding this verse:

علمه اسم كل شيء هذا جبل وهذا بحر وهذا كذا وهذا كذا لكل شيء

He taught him the name of everything, "This is a mountain, this is an ocean, this is so-and-so, this is such-and-such," for every single thing. [53]

[52] *Tafsīr al-Khāzin, Sūrah al-Baqarah: 31*

[53] *Tafsīr al-Ṭabarī, Sūrah al-Baqarah: 31*

Shaykh 'Ismā`īl Ḥaqqī, may Allāh have mercy upon him, mentions that along with the names of all things, Sayyidunā 'Ādam, upon him be salutations, was informed of the religious and worldly benefits of all these things. He further details that he was taught the names of all Angels, all humans, all towns, all villages, and all forms of labor. He was even taught the names of all the bounties of Paradise.[54]

It has even been said that Sayyidunā 'Ādam, upon him be salutations, was given the knowledge of all languages that would come to be.[55] Moreover, one statement of the *mufassirūn* states:

اسم ما كان وما يكون إلى يوم القيامة

[He was taught] The name of all that has been and will be until the Day of Resurrection. [56]

A point to be noted is that if this is the treasure of knowledge that was granted to Sayyidunā 'Ādam, upon him be salutations, then one cannot even begin to imagine the vast oceans of knowledge and wisdom which flow in the pure chest of Sayyidunā Muḥammad al-Muṣṭafā, may Allāh send blessings and salutations upon him.

[54] *Tafsīr Rūḥ al-Bayān, Sūrah al-Baqarah: 31*

[55] *Tafsīr al-Khāzin, Sūrah al-Baqarah: 31*

[56] *Tafsīr al-Maẓharī, Sūrah al-Baqarah: 31*

Despite recognizing such a grand rank of knowledge for Sayyidunā 'Ādam, upon him be salutations, the Noble *'Imām* of the *'Ahl al-Sunnah*, 'Imām 'Aḥmad Riḍā', may Allāh have mercy upon him, erupting with love for the Master of all Prophets, may Allāh send blessings and salutations upon him, says:

فعلوم آدم وعلوم العالم وعلوم اللوح وعلوم القلم كلها

قطرة من بحار علوم حبيبنا صلى الله تعالى عليه وسلم

All knowledge of 'Ādam, all the knowledge of the universe, all knowledge of the sacred tablet, and all the knowledge of the sacred pen, in its totality, is a single drop from the oceans of our Beloved's, may Allāh send blessings and salutations upon him, knowledges. [57]

Nevertheless, it was this caliber in knowledge by which Allāh Almighty manifested the superiority of His *khalīfah* above the congregation of the *Malā'ikah*. The objects whose names had been taught to Sayyidunā 'Ādam, upon him be salutations, were presented unto the *Malā'ikah* and they confessed their inability to name them.

However, when asked the same of Sayyidunā 'Ādam, upon him be salutations, he manifested this gift of knowledge granted to him and his superiority above the *Malā'ikah*.

[57] *al-Dawlah al-Makkīyah bi al-Māddah al-Ghaybīyah: Khuṭbah*

4

PROSTRATING TO SAYYIDUNA 'ADAM

After Allāh Almighty had manifested the superiority of Sayyidunā 'Ādam, upon him be salutations, and the Angels had confessed to this superiority, Allāh Almighty commanded the *Malā'ikah* to perform *sajdah* to Sayyidunā 'Ādam, upon him be salutations.

This occurrence and the events which were to unfold after this divine command are mentioned in the Noble *Qur'ān*:

وَإِذْ قُلْنَا لِلْمَلَٰٓئِكَةِ ٱسْجُدُوا۟ لِءَادَمَ فَسَجَدُوٓا۟ إِلَّآ إِبْلِيسَ أَبَىٰ وَٱسْتَكْبَرَ وَكَانَ مِنَ ٱلْكَٰفِرِينَ

And [remember] when We said to the Angels, "Prostrate to 'Ādam." So, they prostrated, except 'Iblīs. He denied and was arrogant and became of the disbelievers. [58]

[58] *Sūrah al-Baqarah: 34*

In this verse, it is seen that Allāh Almighty once again bestows unto Sayyidunā 'Ādam, upon him be salutations, yet another means of superiority above the Angels. In this occurrence, Allāh Almighty commands all of the Angels to prostrate to Sayyidunā 'Ādam, upon him be salutations.

As followers of Muḥammadan Law, the believers of today reserve the placing of their head on the ground solely for the worship and reverence of Allāh Almighty and for none other does the Muslim so much as bow. Hence, arises the question: why were the Angels commanded to prostrate to Sayyidunā 'Ādam, upon him be salutations?

First and foremost, it must be known that the *sajdah* is of two types:

1) *Sajdah Ta`abbudī*: This is the prostration of worship – to prostrate to someone considering them the creator.
2) *Sajdah Ta`ẓīmī/Taḥīyah*: This prostration is an expression of respect or reverence – to perform *sajdah* to something or someone not considering them to be worthy of worship, but as a form of respect.[59]

To perform *sajdah ta`abbudī* to any other than Allāh Almighty is an act of polytheism; it is *shirk* and has not been permitted in the law of any Prophet.[60]

[59] *Tafsīr Na`īmī, Sūrah al-Baqarah: 34*
[60] *ibid*

Therefore, there is a consensus of the Muslims that the *sajdah* commanded here was not one of worship.[61]

On the other hand, *sajdah ta`ẓīmī* was permitted prior to Muḥammadan Law and an example of such is seen in the brothers of Sayyidunā Yūsuf, upon him be salutations, prostrating to him.[62] In the glorious religion of *'Islām*, it is even prohibited to bow to another in showing respect; if one bows to the extent of *rukū`* in greeting someone, they have acted contrary to the blessed *sharī`ah*.

Such is evident in the writings of the *faqīh* (jurist), Ṣadr al-Sharī`ah Muftī 'Amjad `Alī al-'A`ẓamī, may Allāh have mercy upon him. He writes:

بعض لوگ سلام کرتے وقت جھک بھی جاتے ہیں یہ جھکنا اگر حد رکوع تک ہو تو حرام ہے
اور اس سے کم ہو تو مکروہ ہے

Some people also bow at the time of saying salām – if this bowing is to the extent of rukū`, it is ḥarām (forbidden), and if it is less than this, it is makrūh (disliked). [63]

[61] *Tafsīr Kabīr, Sūrah al-Baqarah: 34*

[62] *Tafsīr Na`īmī, Sūrah al-Baqarah: 34*

[63] *Bahār e Sharī`at, Vol. 16, Salām ka Bayān*

Bowing is impermissible in the *sharī`ah* whether it is done at the time of saying *salām* or upon meeting someone as practiced in certain cultures. *Bahār e Sharī`at* also says:

ملاقات کے وقت جھکنا منع ہے یعنی اتنا جھکنا کہ حد رکوع تک ہو جائے

To bow at the time of greeting is impermissible. In other words, to bow so much that it reaches the extent of rukū`. [64]

Moreover, in this text it is also highlighted that such an expression of reverence is not even permissible in the august court of the most superior creation of Allāh, peace and blessing be upon him:

روضۂ انور کا نہ طواف کرو نہ سجدہ نہ اتنا جھکنا کہ رکوع کے برابر ہو رسول اللہ صلی اللہ تعالی علیہ وسلم کی تعظیم
ان کی اطاعت میں ہے

Do not circumambulate the luminous rawḍah, prostrate to it, nor bow so much that it meets the level of rukū`. Revering the Messenger of Allāh, may Allāh, the Exalted, send blessing upon him and salutation, is within his obedience. [65]

It must be noted however, that if one seems to be bowing for some other purpose as a form of respect, such as lowering oneself for the purpose of kissing the hands or feet of a pious individual or one's own parents, it is permissible.[66]

[64] *Bahār e Sharī`at, Vol. 16, Muṣāfaḥah wa Mu`ānaqah wa Bosah wa Qiyām ka Bayān*

[65] *Bahār e Sharī`at, Vol. 6, Ḥāḍirī Sarkār 'A`ẓam...*

[66] *Tafsīr Na`īmī, Sūrah al-Baqarah: 34*

Unfortunately, some individuals who consider themselves to be above the law of Allāh Almighty engage in this impermissible act of prostrating to others as a form of respect. This, for certain, is not permissible and those who engage in such acts should consider the consequences of disobeying the law of Sayyidunā Rasūl Allāh, may Allāh send blessings and salutations upon him.

When the Noble *Ṣaḥābah*, Allāh is pleased with them, witnessed a tree and a camel prostrating to the Noble Messenger, may Allāh send blessings and salutations upon him, the *Ṣaḥābah*, Allāh is pleased with them, expressed their heart's desire of wishing to do the same while saying:

نحن أولى بالسجود لك من الشجرة والجمل الشارد

We are more deserving of prostrating to you than the tree and the helpless camel.

The Noble Messenger of Allāh, may Allāh send blessings and salutations upon him, responded:

لا ينبغي أن يسجد لأحد إلا لله رب العالمين

One should not prostrate to any but Allāh, the Lord of All Worlds. [67]

[67] *Tafsīr al-Qurṭubī, Sūrah al-Baqarah: 34*

Furthermore, when Sayyidunā Mu`ādh bin Jabal, Allāh is pleased with him, returned from *Shām*, he prostrated to the Messenger of Allāh, may Allāh send blessings and salutations upon him, and thereupon, Sayyidunā Rasūl Allāh, may Allāh send blessings and salutations upon him, exclaimed:

ما هذا

What is this?

Sayyidunā Mu`ādh, Allāh is pleased with him, humbly responded:

يا رسول الله قدمت الشام فرأيتهم يسجدون لبطارقتهم وأساقفتهم فأردت أن أفعل ذلك بك

O Messenger of Allāh, I visited Shām and I saw them prostrating to their patricians and their bishops, so I desired that I do such to you.

The Messenger of Allāh, may Allāh send blessings and salutations upon him, then said:

فلا تفعل فإني لو أمرت شيئا أن يسجد لشيء لأمرت المرأة أن تسجد لزوجها

Do not do so. For, indeed, had I commanded anything to prostrate to another thing, I would have commanded the woman to prostrate to her husband.[68]

[68] *ibid*

The undying and unconditional love for the Noble Messenger, may Allāh send blessings and salutations upon him, in the hearts of the *Ṣaḥābah,* Allāh is pleased with them, nested this desire of prostrating to him as a form of reverence, but after learning of its being forbidden, the *Ṣaḥābah,* Allāh is pleased with them, did not enact this desire. The *sajdah,* of all forms, is reserved for Allāh Almighty in the divine law of *'Islām.*

The *sajdah* to Sayyidunā 'Ādam, upon him be salutations, by which the *Malā'ikah* can be seen being commanded here, however, takes place in a time wherein the Muḥammadan Law had not yet abrogated the *sajdah ta`ẓīmī* and thus, there are three views regarding the nature of this prostration:

1) This *sajdah* was one of worship to Allāh Almighty and Sayyidunā 'Ādam, upon him be salutations, was only made the direction for the *sajdah* as the *Ka`bah* is the direction for the prostration of the believers today; the Muslims pray to Allāh Almighty but face the *Ka`bah* in doing so.
2) This *sajdah* was to Sayyidunā 'Ādam, upon him be salutations, himself as a form of honor and reverence, the equivalent of saying *salām* to him.
3) The word *sajdah* is being used in its literal meaning of obedience or humility; the Angels only expressed humility and obedience in the court of Sayyidunā 'Ādam, upon him be salutations, and this was done without placing their foreheads on the ground.

Amongst these three views, the first position is flawed due to the fact that this command of Allāh Almighty was given to manifest the superiority of Sayyidunā 'Ādam, upon him be salutations, and in such a situation, it is not necessary that the one being prostrated to is superior to the one performing the *sajdah*. This is seen in the fact that Sayyidunā Rasūl Allāh, may Allāh send blessings and salutations upon him, prostrated in the direction of the *Ka`bah* despite being far superior to it.[69] Sayyidunā 'Ādam, upon him be salutations, solely being the direction of the *sajdah* to Allāh Almighty does not manifest his superiority to the *Malā'ikah*.

As for the third position, it is also flawed due to it being apparent that in the *sharī`ah*, the word *sajdah* denotes placing one's head on the ground and thus, it is necessary that the word be left to this original meaning in this case.[70]

The first to submit to the divine will of Allāh Almighty in this grand display of reverence to Sayyidunā 'Ādam, upon him be salutations, was Sayyidunā Jibrīl, upon him be salutations. Thereafter, it was Sayyidunā Mīkā'īl, upon him be salutations, then Sayyidunā 'Isrāfīl, upon him be salutations, then Sayyidunā `Izrā'īl, upon him be salutations, and then the remainder of the beloved *Malā'ikah*, upon them be salutations, prostrated to him.[71]

[69] *Khazā'in al-`Irfān, Sūrah al-Baqarah: 34*

[70] *Tafsīr Kabīr, Sūrah al-Baqarah: 34*

[71] *Khazā'in al-`Irfān, Sūrah al-Baqarah: 34*

This *sajdah* took place on the blessed day of *Jumu`ah* and continued from the start time of *Ẓuhr* up until the time of *`Aṣr*. One position regarding the duration of the *sajdah* states that this *sajdah* lasted one hundred years and another says that it lasted five hundred years.[72]

The way to make all three positions concur with one another is to say that first, the Angels prostrated to Sayyidunā 'Ādam, upon him be salutations, and *Shayṭān* protested doing so. This *sajdah* lasted a short while and the *Malā'ikah* saw 'Iblīs standing with his back turned to Sayyidunā 'Ādam, upon him be salutations, in protest, so the *Malā'ikah* returned to a *sajdah* of gratitude to Allāh Almighty to thank Him for being granted the honor of being able to prostrate to Sayyidunā 'Ādam, upon him be salutations. This second *sajdah* was for Allāh Almighty. Upon rising from this second prostration, the *Malā'ikah* witnessed that the face of 'Iblīs, which was very attractive prior to this display of arrogance, had become disfigured. His body was made to resemble that of a swine and his face resembled an ape. Thereupon, the *Malā'ikah* returned to a third *sajdah* due to the fear of Allāh's punishment. All three of these prostrations were performed in the direction of Sayyidunā 'Ādam, upon him be salutations, but they varied in types and durations.[73]

[72] *ibid*

[73] *Tafsīr Na`īmī, Sūrah al-Baqarah: 34*

In the previously mentioned verse, alongside the honor and reverence of Sayyidunā 'Ādam, upon him be salutations, being demonstrated, the misfortune and the evil nature of *Shayṭān* rises to the surface. He disobeyed the command of Allāh Almighty and exhibited arrogance in the majestic court of the Sole Owner of the Rights to Pride, *al-Mutakabbir*. The grave sin of arrogance became 'Iblīs' means to *kufr*.

He, who was once a pious individual, was bestowed the freedom of journeying throughout the skies and lands and was sent to Earth in leadership of innocent and infallible Angels, was being stripped of all of these bounties, and it was his arrogance which allowed these bounties to be stripped of him.

This, surely, is a lesson for the arrogant. One should always be thankful of Allāh's bounties and consider their attainment solely a result of Allāh's divine mercy and not the result of one's own efforts; if Allāh Almighty wills to take them away, then He may do so without requiring the pleasure or permission of even a single soul. Arrogance can lead one down the road of *kufr* and may thus lead one to eternal punishment.

This incident is detailed in various other sections of the Holy *Qur'ān*. Allāh Almighty details this occurrence and says:

وَلَقَدْ خَلَقْنَٰكُمْ ثُمَّ صَوَّرْنَٰكُمْ ثُمَّ قُلْنَا لِلْمَلَٰٓئِكَةِ اسْجُدُوا لِآدَمَ فَسَجَدُوٓا إِلَّآ إِبْلِيسَ لَمْ يَكُن مِّنَ
السَّٰجِدِينَ ۝ قَالَ مَا مَنَعَكَ أَلَّا تَسْجُدَ إِذْ أَمَرْتُكَ قَالَ أَنَا۠ خَيْرٌ مِّنْهُ خَلَقْتَنِى مِن نَّارٍ وَخَلَقْتَهُۥ
مِن طِينٍ ۝ قَالَ فَاهْبِطْ مِنْهَا فَمَا يَكُونُ لَكَ أَن تَتَكَبَّرَ فِيهَا فَاخْرُجْ إِنَّكَ مِنَ الصَّٰغِرِينَ ۝

And surely, We have created you and molded you. Then, We said to the Angels, "Prostrate to 'Ādam." So, they all prostrated except 'Iblīs. He was not of those who prostrated. He said, "What prevented you that you did not prostrate when I commanded you?" He said, "I am better than him. You created me from fire, and You created him from clay." He said, "Descend from here. It is not for you to stay here and be arrogant. Leave! Surely, you are of the humiliated." [74]

These verses of the Noble *Qur'ān* clarify what exactly it was that caused the wretched *Shayṭān* to be boastful of himself and what led the most inferior being to think of himself as superior to Sayyidunā 'Ādam, upon him be salutations.

He had become victim to the false notion that fire was superior to soil and, as a result, he thought that he should be superior to Sayyidunā 'Ādam, upon him be salutations. This perception of his was itself erroneous.

[74] *Sūrah al-'A`rāf: 11-13*

Superior is he who Allāh Almighty grants superiority and the basis of superiority is not upon one's essence, rather, it is upon piety and obedience to the Creator Almighty.

Moreover, 'Iblīs had already erred in thinking that the fire is superior to soil. Fire bears qualities of rage and rising, both being means to arrogance. On the other hand, by the means of soil, one is led to dignity, forbearance, humility, and patience. Good soil is a magnet for communities to come and populate a land and fire destroys communities.

Soil is trustworthy as it nurtures growth, safeguards that which is placed in it, and allows it to grow, and that which is placed in fire meets its end. Moreover, soil extinguishes fire whereas fire cannot destroy soil.

Despite the reality being so evident that soil is superior to fire, 'Iblīs manifests a lack of intelligence and takes a leap towards his doom. The greatest display of ignorance was actually in relying upon reason and rationale in the presence of a command coming from Allāh Almighty. Any ruling given based upon reason while opposing the command of Allāh Almighty and His Messenger, may Allāh send blessings and salutations upon him, will surely be a means of destruction and will be unacceptable.[75]

[75] *Khazā'in al-`Irfān, Sūrah al-'A`rāf: 12*

The series of events which unfolded following this display of arrogance are detailed in the latter verses:

قَالَ أَنظِرْنِي إِلَىٰ يَوْمِ يُبْعَثُونَ ۝ قَالَ إِنَّكَ مِنَ الْمُنظَرِينَ ۝ قَالَ فَبِمَا أَغْوَيْتَنِي لَأَقْعُدَنَّ لَهُمْ
صِرَاطَكَ الْمُسْتَقِيمَ ۝ ثُمَّ لَآتِيَنَّهُم مِّن بَيْنِ أَيْدِيهِمْ وَمِنْ خَلْفِهِمْ وَعَنْ أَيْمَانِهِمْ وَعَن شَمَائِلِهِمْ
وَلَا تَجِدُ أَكْثَرَهُمْ شَاكِرِينَ ۝ قَالَ اخْرُجْ مِنْهَا مَذْءُومًا مَّدْحُورًا لَّمَن تَبِعَكَ مِنْهُمْ لَأَمْلَأَنَّ
جَهَنَّمَ مِنكُمْ أَجْمَعِينَ ۝

He said, "Grant me respite to the day they will be resurrected." He said, "Indeed, you are of those granted respite." He said, "I swear by Your misguiding me, I will surely sit in wait for them on Your straight path. Then, surely, I will approach them from in front of them, behind them, from their right sides, and their left sides. You will not find most of them to be grateful." He said, "Leave from here rejected, expelled! Indeed, whomsoever of them is obedient to you, I will surely fill hell of you all." [76]

It is seen in these verses that despite a horrid display of audacity in the majestic court of Allāh Almighty, 'Iblīs continues to dig himself deeper in the burrow of painful torment and asks Allāh Almighty for respite in roaming the lands to misguide His slaves. The duration of this respite has been mentioned to be up until the first blow of the horn by which all people will die.

[76] *Sūrah al-'A'rāf: 14-18*

Initially, as seen in this verse, 'Iblīs had sought respite to the time wherein the dead are resurrected seeking to escape the torturous claws of death, but this ask was not fulfilled and he was given respite only until the first blow of the horn.[77]

This is seen in *Sūrah al-Ḥijr*:

قَالَ رَبِّ فَأَنۡظِرۡنِيۡۤ اِلٰى يَوۡمِ يُبۡعَثُوۡنَ ۝ قَالَ فَاِنَّكَ مِنَ الۡمُنۡظَرِيۡنَ ۝ اِلٰى يَوۡمِ الۡوَقۡتِ الۡمَعۡلُوۡمِ ۝

He said, "My Lord, grant me respite until the day they are resurrected." He said, "You are of those granted respite, to the day of the known time." [78]

It was the arrogance that 'Iblīs harbored in his heart and mind which led to his banishment from the majestic court of Allāh Almighty and becoming the accursed enemy of man until the end of existence.

Upon being banished from this majestic court, Allāh Almighty poured upon him showers of His wrath and also said:

قَالَ فَاخۡرُجۡ مِنۡهَا فَاِنَّكَ رَجِيۡمٌ ۝ وَّاِنَّ عَلَيۡكَ اللَّعۡنَةَ اِلٰى يَوۡمِ الدِّيۡنِ ۝

He said, "Be gone from here for indeed, you are accursed! And, indeed, upon you is the curse until the Day of Resurrection." [79]

[77] *Khazā'in al-`Irfān, Sūrah al-'A`rāf: 15*

[78] *Sūrah al-Ḥijr: 36-38*

[79] *Sūrah al-Ḥijr: 34-35*

'Iblīs fell into the pit of his doom and will be cursed to the Day of *Qiyāmah* by the dwellers of the sky and of the land and with this curse, he will be held captive in eternal punishment from which there is no escape.

Furthermore, the reality is that his corrupt nature does not wish an escape from the torment of the hellfire as to this day, he bears no remorse for his actions and has no will to rectify his doings.

Referencing a *ḥadīth*, Shaykh 'Ismā`īl Ḥaqqī, may Allāh have mercy upon him, states that in *Qiyāmah*, after being held captive in hell for the duration of one thousand years, *Shayṭān* will be taken out and will be made to stand before Sayyidunā 'Ādam, upon him be salutations. Thereupon, he will once again be commanded to prostrate to Sayyidunā 'Ādam, upon him be salutations. He will disobey yet again and be thrown into the hellfire eternally.[80]

Shayṭān feels no remorse for his deeds, and he is still not ready to exhibit respect in the court of Sayyidunā 'Ādam, upon him be salutations.

In the time of Sayyidunā Mūsā, upon him be salutations, *Shayṭān* approached his presence and said, "O Mūsā, you are the one Allāh selected for His messenger-hood and He spoke to you directly. I have sinned and I intend to repent. So, intercede on my behalf to my Lord that He accepts my repentance."

[80] *Tafsīr Rūḥ al-Bayān, Sūrah al-Baqarah: 34*

Sayyidunā Mūsā, upon him be salutations, responded, "Sure."

Thereafter, Sayyidunā Mūsā, upon him be salutations, supplicated to his Lord Almighty and it was said to him, "O Mūsā, I have fulfilled your need."

Sayyidunā Mūsā, upon him be salutations, met with 'Iblīs and said, "He has commanded that you prostrate to the grave of 'Ādam [out of respect] and your repentance will be accepted."

'Iblīs, once again, exhibited arrogance and became infuriated and said, "I did not prostrate to him while he was alive, will I prostrate to him after he has passed?"[81]

It can be seen here that even though 'Iblīs expresses the desire to be forgiven, he is still not ready to show any respect to Sayyidunā 'Ādam, upon him be salutations, and Allāh Almighty is not willing to accept him while he harbors animosity for someone beloved to Him Almighty. There is a great lesson in this entire occurrence for those pseudo *Salafīs* who claim to bear the flag for the doctrine of *Tawḥīd* while harboring animosity for he who is the Most Beloved of Allāh, may Allāh send blessings and salutations upon him.

Likewise, the treacherous reject approached Sayyidunā Nūh, upon him be salutations, when he ascended the ark. 'Iblīs approached him and Sayyidunā Nūḥ, upon him be salutations, asked, "Who are you?"

[81] *al-Durr al-Manthūr, Sūrah al-Baqarah: 34*

He responded, "I am 'Iblīs."

Sayyidunā Nūḥ, upon him be salutations, said, "What brings you here?"

'Iblīs responded, "I have come so that you ask my Lord whether there is any repentance for me." Thereupon, Allāh Almighty revealed to Sayyidunā Nūḥ, upon him be salutations, "His repentance is that he goes to the grave of 'Ādam and prostrates to it."

'Iblīs, the accursed, responded saying, "Why, I did not prostrate to him while he was alive, and I should do so while he has passed?"[82]

He displayed his arrogant nature once again and made nothing of the chance to repentance. Surely, he will meet his fate in the scorching flames of hell.

May Allāh Almighty safeguard us from the sin of arrogance and the treachery of *Shayṭān*.

[82] *ibid*

5

CREATION OF WOMAN

After the *Malā'ikah* had prostrated to Sayyidunā 'Ādam, upon him be salutations, and 'Iblīs had been banished from the majestic court of Allāh Almighty, Sayyidunā 'Ādam, upon him be salutations, sojourned in *Jannah* and enjoyed its amenities.

Although Sayyidunā 'Ādam, upon him be salutations, was living in *Jannah*, he was alone and had no one to keep him company. Allāh Almighty put Sayyidunā 'Ādam, upon him be salutations, to sleep and removed a rib from his left side. From this rib, Allāh Almighty created a wife for Sayyidunā 'Ādam, upon him be salutations. After removing this rib, Allāh Almighty replaced it in his body with flesh.

This entire procedure took place in a manner wherein Sayyidunā ʻĀdam, upon him be salutations, did not feel a thing and nor did he feel a pinch of pain.

Had he felt any pain in this procedure, man would never feel any inclination towards woman.[83]

The fact that the wife of Sayyidunā ʻĀdam, upon him be salutations, was born from him is also seen in the Holy *Qur'ān* as Allāh Almighty says:

يَٰٓأَيُّهَا ٱلنَّاسُ ٱتَّقُوا۟ رَبَّكُمُ ٱلَّذِى خَلَقَكُم مِّن نَّفْسٍ وَٰحِدَةٍ
وَخَلَقَ مِنْهَا زَوْجَهَا وَبَثَّ مِنْهُمَا رِجَالًا كَثِيرًا وَنِسَآءً

O people, fear your Lord, the One who created you all from a single soul, created from it its spouse, and spread from them two a plethora of men and women. [84]

Allāh Almighty mentions in this part of the verse that the root of mankind's entirety is one soul, Sayyidunā ʻĀdam, upon him be salutations, and that it is this very life from which stemmed his spouse.

The fact that the wife of Sayyidunā ʻĀdam, upon him be salutations, was born from a part of his own body may lead to the assumption that this was a means of deficiency or flaw in Sayyidunā ʻĀdam, upon him be salutations, as a part of his body is being removed.

[83] *Tafsīr al-Khāzin, Sūrah al-Baqarah: 35*

[84] *Sūrah al-Nisā': 1*

However, this is not the case and the removal of a part from his body, in reality, was a means to his perfection. The creation of a spouse gave him peace and the unease of solitude was removed from him because of her.[85]

Having a pious wife is superior to many bounties of life. Man may be afflicted with unnumbered difficulties, but if he finds ease and solace from his wife, he finds the courage to battle his hardships. However, if man does not find peace within his own spouse, no matter the lavish lifestyle and unimaginable bounties he has been granted, he will always find it difficult to attain solace. This is seen in the statement of the Noble Messenger, may Allāh send blessings and salutations upon him, as he states:

الدنيا متاع وخير متاع الدنيا المرأة الصالحة

The world is a commodity, and the most superior commodity of the world is a righteous woman. [86]

Upon awakening from his sleep, Sayyidunā 'Ādam, upon him be salutations, found her to be seated at his head side and he asked her, "Who are you?"

She responded, "A woman."

"Why have you been created?" he inquired.

[85] *Tafsīr Rūḥ al-Bayān, Sūrah al-Baqarah: 35*

[86] *Ṣaḥīḥ Muslim: 715k*

She replied, "For you to find peace in me."[87]

In another account of this incident, she added the words, "and for me to find peace in you."[88]

At this time, the *Malā'ikah*, seeking another opportunity to witness the unmatched knowledge Allāh Almighty had bestowed upon Sayyidunā 'Ādam, upon him be salutations, asked him, "What is her name?"

To this, Sayyidunā 'Ādam, upon him be salutations, responded, "Ḥawwā'."

"Why has she been named Ḥawwā'?" the *Malā'ikah* inquired.

Sayyidunā 'Ādam, upon him be salutations, said, "Because she has been created from a *ḥayy* (living being)."[89]

Having been created from a part of Sayyidunā 'Ādam, upon him be salutations, her name itself, Ḥawwā', was derived from the word "*ḥayy*" which denotes a living being.

According to a different account of this incident, the reason for her being named Ḥawwā' was that she is the origin for every *ḥayy*, all living people.[90]

[87] *Tafsīr Kabīr, Sūrah al-Baqarah: 35*

[88] *Tafsīr al-Khāzin, Sūrah al-Baqarah: 35*

[89] *Tafsīr al-Qurṭubī, Sūrah al-Baqarah: 35*

[90] *Tafsīr Rūḥ al-Bayān, Sūrah al-Baqarah: 35*

In this first meeting amongst the honorable father and mother of all of mankind, the *Malā'ikah* asked, "Do you love her O 'Ādam?"

Sayyidunā 'Ādam, upon him be salutations, responded, "Yes."

The same was then asked of Sayyidatunā Ḥawwā', Allāh is pleased with her, and she responded, "No," despite possessing a depth of affection far greater than what he possessed of love.

Upon hearing this response, the *Malā'ikah* said, "If any woman speaks the reality regarding her love for her husband, then Ḥawwā' has surely told the reality."[91]

This incident speaks volumes regarding the true nature and natural disposition of woman. Sayyidatunā Ḥawwā', Allāh is pleased with her, possessed great love for her husband but was unable to express it in words and this was due to the immense modesty Allāh Almighty has instilled in the disposition of woman. Many a time, while the woman loves her husband, she is unable to express it in words and thus, strives to express this love in forms other than spoken word.

Moreover, it should be noted that this is not a display of such a pious woman telling a lie, as a pious wife of a Prophet would not be imagined to be telling a lie. Rather, this is a display of her bashfulness, and it is a model for the women to come regarding how they shall conceal the private and intimate matters shared between man and wife.

9. *ibid*

Learning of this incident only emphasizes the exemplary modesty and shyness possessed by Sayyidatunā Ḥawwā', Allāh is pleased with her.

Following this initial sight of Sayyidatunā Ḥawwā', Allāh is pleased with her, Sayyidunā 'Ādam, upon him be salutations, sought to seek solace in her and extended his hand towards her. Seeing this, the *Malā'ikah* exclaimed, "Stop O 'Ādam!"

"Why, when Allāh has created her for me?" he responded.

The *Malā'ikah* said, "Only until you pay her *mahr* (dowry)."

Sayyidunā 'Ādam, upon him be salutations, inquired, "What is her *mahr*?"

They said, "That you send *ṣalāh* upon Muḥammad, may Allāh send blessings and salutations upon him, three times."

According to another narration, it was twenty times.[92]

At last, he approached her lovingly saying:

لحمی ودمی وزوجتی

My flesh, my blood, my wife! [93]

These narrations all indicate that Sayyidatunā Ḥawwā', Allāh is pleased with her, was brought to life in *Jannah* whereas some narrations mention an alternative view in this matter.

[92] *al-'Anwār al-Muḥammadīyah, al-Maqṣad al-'Awwal*

[93] *Tafsīr al-Ṭabarī, Sūrah al-Baqarah: 35*

This other position suggests that she was born on Earth and raised to *Jannah* thereafter.

According to this view, Allāh Almighty sent an army of *Malā'ikah* to escort Sayyidunā 'Ādam, upon him be salutations, and Sayyidatunā Ḥawwā', Allāh is pleased with her, on a throne of gold. They were clothed in light and on each of the two was a crown of gold embellished with gems and pearls. After being adorned in such a manner, they were escorted into *Jannah*.[94]

Both of these positions are attributed to two schools of the Noble *Ṣaḥābah*, Allāh is pleased with them, and Allāh Almighty knows best of the reality.

In conclusion, Sayyidunā 'Ādam, upon him be salutations, and Sayyidatunā Ḥawwā', Allāh is pleased with her, were both commanded to dwell in *Jannah* as Allāh Almighty said:

وَقُلْنَا يَٰٓـَٔادَمُ ٱسْكُنْ أَنتَ وَزَوْجُكَ ٱلْجَنَّةَ وَكُلَا مِنْهَا رَغَدًا حَيْثُ شِئْتُمَا
وَلَا تَقْرَبَا هَٰذِهِ ٱلشَّجَرَةَ فَتَكُونَا مِنَ ٱلظَّٰلِمِينَ

And We said, "O 'Ādam sojourn, you and your wife, in Jannah, and eat from it freely as you wish, but do not approach this tree lest you be from amongst those who transgress." [95]

Note: The word "*ẓālim*" used in this verse is derived from the word "*ẓulm*" which denotes the placement of something in a place not meant for it.

[94] *Tafsīr Kabīr, Sūrah al-Baqarah: 35*

[95] *Sūrah al-Baqarah: 35*

This is an impermissible act, and the Noble Prophets, upon them be salutations, are infallible. Thus, in this verse, "*ẓulm*" entails an act performed contrary to the preferred (*khilāf al-'awlā*).

To deem any Prophet a *ẓālim* is surely blasphemy and *kufr*. He who utters such words will be deemed a *kāfir*. Allāh Almighty is the Creator and the Supreme, He says what He wills, but this does not give any other the right to bring a word of disrespect for the Prophets, upon them be salutations, on their tongue, and nor does this statement of Allāh Almighty give anyone the right to audacious statements in the majestic courts of the Prophets, upon them be salutations.

The believers are commanded to always revere the status of the Prophets, upon them be salutations, and to honor them.[96]

Moreover, in this verse of the Noble *Qur'ān*, while commanding the stay in *Jannah*, Allāh Almighty says, "*'Uskun.*" This word is derived from the word "*suknā*" which means a place of sojourning, a temporary stay, and not a place of permanent residence.[97]

This is foreshadowing the reality which was soon to be revealed that Sayyidunā 'Ādam, upon him be salutations, was created for the Earth and that a day would come wherein he would leave the abode of *Jannah*.

[96] *Khazā'in al-`Irfān, Sūrah al-Baqarah: 35*

[97] *Tafsīr al-Qurṭubī, Sūrah al-Baqarah: 35*

This stay in *Jannah,* alongside the luxury and lavishness of the eternal abode for the believers, included a glimpse to life on Earth wherein the believers would witness many modes of lavishness but would be commanded to abstain from such modes of luxury. Thus, this stay in *Jannah* would prepare Sayyidunā 'Ādam, upon him be salutations, and Sayyidatunā Ḥawwā', Allāh is pleased with her, for the life which was before them.

6

LIFE IN JANNAH

The Noble Parents of Mankind, upon the gracious command of Allāh Almighty, occupied the abode of *Jannah* and enjoyed the luxuries of Paradise. Both, Sayyidunā 'Ādam, upon him be salutations, and Sayyidatunā Ḥawwā', Allāh is pleased with her, were given permission to eat and drink as they pleased. They were bestowed the honor to savor Heaven's bounties, the food and drink for which there is no fear of an end, nor any risk of harm or indigestion.

Alongside the delicacies of *Jannah*, they were given exposure to the provisions of the land as by merely experiencing the foods of *Jannah*, they could not have reaped a complete experience which would prepare them for life on Earth.

By exposure to all such provisions, they were being prepared for their next destination – Earth.[98]

Furthermore, besides being given permission to eat as they wished, they were granted the access to eat wherever they wished in *Jannah*. Every section of Paradise differed in its environment, and their dwellings and castles were all appealing. The opportunity of being able to roam freely in Paradise allowed them to witness the settings in the diverse landscapes, and this was a means for them to learn how they and their offspring shall occupy Earth. These experiences were to act as models in the mind upon which they would develop life on land so that the world would foreshadow, for the dwellers of the Earth, the life of the hereafter.[99]

The Earth itself was to contain many modes of enjoyment and amusement, but the believing men and women would be commanded to restrain themselves from falling into many of the pleasures of Earth and that which their hearts would desire, and thus to experience this as well, they were commanded to refrain from a particular tree. This was the command of Allāh Almighty:

وَلَا تَقْرَبَا هَٰذِهِ الشَّجَرَةَ

And do not approach this tree... [100]

[98] *Tafsīr Na`īmī, Sūrah al-Baqarah: 35*

[99] *ibid*

[100] *Sūrah al-Baqarah: 35*

There is a difference of opinion regarding what kind of tree it was exactly that the Noble Sayyidunā ‘Ādam, upon him be salutations, and Sayyidatunā Ḥawwā’, Allāh is pleased with her, were commanded to refrain from. The position narrated from ‘Imām Mujāhid, may Allāh have mercy upon him, Sa`īd bin Jubayr, may Allāh have mercy upon him, and Sayyidunā `Abd Allāh ‘ibn `Abbās, Allāh is pleased with them, says that this was a tree of wheat. It is also narrated from Sayyidunā `Abd Allāh ‘ibn Mas`ūd, Allāh is pleased with him, and Sayyidunā `Abd Allāh ‘ibn `Abbās, Allāh is pleased with them, that this was a tree of grapes. Another narration of ‘Imām Mujāhid, may Allāh have mercy upon him, and Qatādah, may Allāh have mercy upon him, says that it was a tree of figs.[101]

Anyhow, as the two toured and experienced the wonders of *Jannah*, the malicious ‘Iblīs grew in his jealousy towards Sayyidunā ‘Ādam, upon him be salutations, and the unmatched rank he had been granted. Due to such malice, he kept his eyes open for an opportunity to strip Sayyidunā ‘Ādam, upon him be salutations, of his grandeur. Surely, *Shayṭān* was foolish in thinking that this status of a Prophet can be taken away and thus failed miserably in this mission as the lofty rank of Sayyidunā ‘Ādam, upon him be salutations, remained unstained despite the efforts of ‘Iblīs.[102]

[101] *Tafsīr Kabīr, Sūrah al-Baqarah: 35*

[102] *Tafsīr Rūḥ al-Bayān, Sūrah al-Baqarah: 36*

However, due to his treachery, the time had arrived wherein Sayyidunā 'Ādam, upon him be salutations, would meet his fate of inhabiting Earth and he would have to leave *Jannah* for this purpose.

This is mentioned in the Holy *Qur'ān* as Allāh Almighty states:

فَأَزَلَّهُمَا الشَّيۡطٰنُ عَنۡهَا فَأَخۡرَجَهُمَا مِمَّا كَانَا فِيۡهِ وَقُلۡنَا اهۡبِطُوۡا بَعۡضُكُمۡ لِبَعۡضٍ عَدُوٌّ
وَلَكُمۡ فِي الۡأَرۡضِ مُسۡتَقَرٌّ وَّمَتَاعٌ إِلٰى حِيۡنٍ

So, Shayṭān caused them to slip from Jannah and separated them from where they used to live. And We said, "Descend! One of you is an enemy to another, and for you, in the land, is residence and provision to a time."[103]

Prior to understanding this occurrence, it is incumbent upon the believer to familiarize themselves with the rank and status granted to the Noble Prophets, upon them be salutations. Unfortunately, today is a time wherein the people speak in audacious tones and make bold statements in the majestic courts of the Noble Prophets, upon them be salutations, and present the Noble Prophets, upon them be salutations, as common people prone to sin. However, this is surely not the case, and the Noble Prophets of Allāh, upon them be salutations, are all *ma`ṣūm*; they are infallible, and Allāh Almighty has divinely protected them from the flaw of sinning. This is the doctrine of the *'Ahl al-Sunnah* and the belief of the righteous predecessors.

[103] *Sūrah al-Baqarah: 36*

Manifesting the true creed of *'Islām*, the noble *tābi`ī*, 'Imām 'A`ẓam 'Abū Ḥanīfah, may Allāh have mercy upon him, explicitly states in *al-Fiqh al-'Akbar*:

والأنبياء عليهم الصلوة والسلام كلهم منزهون من الصغائر

والكبائر والكفر والقبائح

The Prophets, upon them be blessing and salutation, each one of them, are pure of the minor sins, the major sins, disbelief, and abominations.[104]

This text clearly mentions that the Noble Prophets, upon them be salutations, do not sin, whether the sin is minor or major; they are pure of all actions which contradict the divine pleasure of Allāh Almighty. However, explaining some of the actions of the Noble Prophets, upon them be salutations, the Noble *'Imām*, may Allāh have mercy upon him, further states:

وقد كانت منهم زلات وخطايا

And occur from them [apparent] missteps and miscalculations. [105]

This portion of the text clarifies that those actions of the Noble Prophets, upon them be salutations, which an unlearned eye may see to be a sin, are not truly sins; they are apparent missteps and miscalculations. Such is the case for that which the accursed *Shayṭān* led Sayyidunā 'Ādam, upon him be salutations, to do.

[104] *al-Fiqh al-'Akbar, al-Qawl fī `Ismah al-'Anbiyā'*

[105] *ibid*

Supporting the position displayed by 'Imām 'A`ẓam 'Abū Ḥanīfah, may Allāh have mercy upon him, 'Imām Kamāl 'ibn Humām, may Allāh have mercy upon him, writes:

والمختار العصمة عنهما

The chosen position is infallibility from both of them (major and minor sins). [106]

In this text, 'Imām 'Ibn Humām, may Allāh have mercy upon him, clarifies, after some discussion, that the position adopted by the majority of the *'Ahl al-Sunnah* is that of the Noble Prophets, upon them be salutations, being infallible in terms of major and minor sins both. This is the position which befits the honorable ranks of the Noble Prophets, upon them be salutations; Allāh Almighty has purified them from the evils of any sin, major or minor.

While 'Imām 'Ibn Humām, may Allāh have mercy upon him, has mentioned the belief of the majority concerning the major and minor sins, the Noble Qāḍī `Iyāḍ, may Allāh have mercy upon him, displays the consensus of all believers regarding the belief of attributing to the Noble Prophets, upon them be salutations, the major sins, those which necessitate any punishment, and all forms of obscenities.

[106] *al-Musāyarah, al-Rukn al-Thālith*

He writes:

فأجمع المسلمون على عصمة الأنبياء من الفواحش والكبائر الموبقات

All Muslims have consensually agreed upon the infallibility of the Prophets from all obscenities and the destructive major sins. [107]

Further into his renowned *al-Shifā'*, the Noble Qāḍī `Iyāḍ, may Allāh have mercy upon him, pens a chapter in refutation of those scholars who are of the view that although the Noble Prophets, upon them be salutations, are infallible in terms of *kufr* and the major sins, the occurrence of minor sins on their behalf is possible. In this chapter, he also explains that the Noble Prophets, upon them be salutations, are infallible in terms of minor sins as well and that this is the more accurate position in this regard.[108]

While it is now clear as day that the adopted position of the *'Ahl al-Sunnah* is that the Noble Prophets, upon them be salutations, are infallible in terms of both major and minor sins, the intellect seeks a way to make sense of various reports regarding the actions of the Noble and Infallible Prophets, upon them be salutations, of Allāh Almighty which one could misconstrue as a sin.

[107] *al-Shifā', al-Juz' al-Thānī, al-Bāb al-'Awwal fī mā Yakhstaṣṣu bi al-'Umūr al-Dīnīyah wa al-Kalām fī `Ismah Nabīyinā, al-Faṣl al-Tāsi`*

[108] *al-Shifā', al-Juz' al-Thānī, al-Bāb al-'Awwal fī mā Yakhstaṣṣu bi al-'Umūr al-Dīnīyah wa al-Kalām fī `Ismah Nabīyinā, al-Faṣl al-Thālith `Ashar*

The procedure of dealing with such reports is detailed by the Honorable Author of *Sharḥ al-`Aqā'id al-Nasafīyah*, 'Imām Sa`d al-Dīn al-Taftāzānī, may Allāh have mercy upon him:

فما نقل عن الأنبياء عليهم السلام مما يشعر بكذب أو معصية فما كان منقولا بطريق الآحاد فمردود وما كان بطريق التواتر مصروف عن ظاهره إن أمكن وإلا فمحمول على ترك الأولى أو كونه قبل البعثة

So, whatever is reported regarding the Prophets, upon them be salutations, *from what can be perceived as a lie or as disobedience, whatever is reported by way of solitary reports is rejected. Whatever is [reported] by way of mass-transmission will be turned away from its outward appearance if it is possible. Otherwise, it will be applied on leaving that which is preferable or it being before [declaring] prophethood.* [109]

Adhering to this method of dealing with such reports, the Noble Scholars of the *'Ahl al-Sunnah* have explained the verses which relate to that which was carried out by Sayyidunā 'Ādam, upon him be salutations.

Ṣadr al-'Afāḍil Sayyid Na`īm al-Dīn Murādābādī, may Allāh have mercy upon him, explains that Sayyidunā 'Ādam, upon him be salutations, had perceived the prohibition of eating from the tree as *tanzīhī* (restriction of dislike) and not as *taḥrīmī* (prohibitive restriction).

[109] *Sharḥ al-`Aqā'id, al-'Anbiyā' Ma`ṣūmūn*

Had Sayyidunā 'Ādam, upon him be salutations, believed it to be a prohibitive restriction, he would have never eaten from the tree due to his infallibility.

He further explains that this was a miscalculation in his judgment (*khaṭa' 'ijtihādī*) and a miscalculation of this kind is not a sin.[110]

An alternative explanation is presented by `Allāmah Mullā `Alī Qārī, may Allāh have mercy upon him, wherein he locates the miscalculation of Sayyidunā 'Ādam, upon him be salutations, to be in the fact that he thought that Allāh Almighty had placed a restriction on the approaching of one tree in particular whereas Allāh Almighty had placed this restriction on that particular type of tree. Thus, he ate not from that exact tree, he ate from another tree of the same type. Moreover, Mullā `Alī Qārī, may Allāh have mercy upon him, explains that all of this was from the magnificent wisdoms of Allāh Almighty and this was done to make manifest the weakness of man and his need for the forgiveness of Allāh Almighty.

[110] *Khazā'in al-`Irfān, Sūrah al-Baqarah: 36*

Furthermore, he relates this explanation to a *ḥadīth*, wherein it is stated:

لولم تذنبوا لجاء الله بقوم يذنبون فيستغفرون فيغفر الله لهم

Had you not committed mistakes, Allāh would bring a people who commit mistakes. They would ask forgiveness and Allāh would forgive them. [111]

This shows that this incident is not one for the people to raise objections against the lofty status of the Prophets, upon them be salutations, rather, it is one from which the people should take the lesson of seeking forgiveness from Allāh Almighty for their own shortcomings and to expect that Allāh Almighty will forgive their wrongs. This is one of the first lessons being given to those who would come from the offspring of Sayyidunā 'Ādam, upon him be salutations: Allāh Almighty is the Oft-Forgiving, and He loves to forgive.

[111] *Sharḥ al-Fiqh al-'Akbar, al-'Anbiyā' Munazzahūn `an al-Ṣaghā'ir wa al-Kabā'ir*

Another verse of the Holy *Qur'ān* that those who harbor animosity for the Noble Prophets, upon them be salutations, use to raise objections against the infallibility of the Prophets, upon them be salutations, is:

وَعَصٰۤی اٰدَمُ رَبَّهٗ فَغَوٰی

And a [apparent] misstep occurred from 'Ādam in the command of his Lord, so he did not find the route of what he intended. [112]

In this verse of the Noble *Qur'ān*, Allāh Almighty used the word "`*aṣā*" to describe the action of Sayyidunā 'Ādam, upon him be salutations. This word is derived from the root of "`*isyān*" which, in the case that it is used for a common man, would translate to a sin or disobedience.

However, bearing the doctrine of infallibility for the Prophets, upon them be salutations, in mind, how could one possibly translate this word as a sin or an act of disobedience? And why is such a word being used to describe the act of a Beloved Prophet, upon him be salutations?

[112] *Sūrah Ṭā-Hā: 121*

The Author of *al-Nibrās*, `Allāmah `Abd al-`Azīz, may Allāh have mercy upon him, writes:

وقال غير واحد من الأئمة سمى الله ترك الأولى منهم عصيانا لعظم منزلتهم كما قيل حسنات الأبرار سيئات المقربين واستغفار من ترك الأولى هضما لنفوسهم وإلا فليس من الذنب ولا عقاب عليه

More than just one of the 'imāms say, "Allāh labels their leaving of the preferred as `iṣyān due to the prominence of their status, comparable to the saying, 'The good deeds of the righteous are shortcomings with respect to the close ones.' The repentance from leaving that which is preferred is to suppress their egos. Otherwise, it is not a sin and nor is there any punishment for it." [113]

This text clarifies that this word being used in the Noble *Qur'ān* by Allāh Almighty is due to the lofty stature of Sayyidunā 'Ādam, upon him be salutations. Had this action been carried out by an ordinary man, it would not be abominable as there is no issue for the common man in leaving that which is preferrable for another that is permissible as well.

However, Sayyidunā 'Ādam, upon him be salutations, is from amongst those who are close to Allāh Almighty and even the good deeds of a common man seem like sins on his scale of piety and righteousness, and thus, this word is being used to describe his action which is going against that which is preferable.

[113] *al-Nibrās, al-'Anbiyā' Ma`ṣūmūn*

Moreover, it is Allāh Almighty who is saying this, and it befits Him to speak to His creation as He wills, but this does not give anyone else the right to speak in the same manner regarding those who are beloved to Allāh Almighty. It is necessary that the believer always practice extreme caution in speaking of the Noble Prophets, upon them be salutations. They must tread as if they walk on a sharp-edged sword; the slightest slip of tongue will not be tolerated.

Accordingly, the Noble Jurist of *'Islām* and the Unmatched Scholar, the *'Imām* of the *'Ahl al-Sunnah* 'Imām 'Aḥmad Riḍā', may Allāh have mercy upon him, states, "In other than the recitation of the *Qur'ān*, attributing disobedience and sin to Sayyidunā 'Ādam, upon him be blessing and salutation, on one's own is *ḥarām*. The *'imāms* of the religion have explicitly stated this. Rather, one group of the noble scholars have said for this to be *kufr*. It befits the Master [Almighty] that in whatever form He may make mention of His beloved servants, He may. [However,] If another were to say it, his tongue shall be snatched from the nape."[114]

Further explaining this concept, the Noble 'Imām, may Allāh have mercy upon him, gives an example without comparison in order to engrave this teaching in the heart and mind of the believer: Imagine if Zayd, while correcting the behavior of his son, `Amr, and training him to practice utmost caution, scolds him and refers to him as an undisciplined and unworthy fool.

[114] *Fatāwā Raḍawīyah, Risālah 'Irtifā` al-Ḥujub `an Wujūh Qirā'ah al-Junub*

Zayd had every right to speak to his son in such a manner. However, if `Amr's son, Bakr, or his servant, Khālid, make these words a basis for them to use for their father or master, they will be deemed disobedient and will be worthy of being punished.

Moreover, if this is the case for this scenario, then why shall the one who makes the word of Allāh Almighty a basis to disrespect those beloved to Allāh Almighty not be worthy of Allāh Almighty's inescapable torment and a victim of His wrath?[115]

'Imām 'Aḥmad Riḍā' al-Baraylawī, may Allāh have mercy upon him, mentions the position of a group from amongst the noble scholars who say that it would be *kufr* to mention such words on one's own behalf for the Noble Prophets, upon them be salutations, outside of reciting the *Qur'ān*, and he quotes 'Imām 'Ibn al-Ḥājj in *Madkhal* while presenting this position.

'Imām 'Ibn al-Ḥājj writes:

قد قال علمائنا رحمهم الله تعالى أن من قال عن نبى من الأنبياء عليهم الصلاة والسلام فى
غير التلاوة والحديث أنه عصى أو خالف فقد كفر نعوذ بالله من ذلك

Our scholars, may Allāh, the Exalted, envelope them in mercy, have said that whoever says regarding any one Prophet from amongst the Prophets, upon them be blessing and salutation, outside of reciting the Qur'ān or ḥadīth, that he has committed `iṣyān or that he has disobeyed, he has committed kufr. We seek refuge with Allāh from that. [116]

[115] *ibid*

[116] *ibid*

This shows that despite the fact that such words have been used to describe the doings of the Noble Prophets, upon them be salutations, by Allāh Almighty in the Holy *Qur'ān*, one is not to attribute such words to the Beloved Prophets, upon them be salutations, on his own. Rather, one will tread cautiously when speaking of the Noble Prophets, upon them be salutations, and pay close attention to his choice of words when doing so. This caution must be practiced even when translating these words of the Noble *Qur'ān*. The status and rank of the Noble Prophets, upon them be salutations, must be kept in sight even then.

It is unfortunate that in a number of the translations of the *Qur'ān* which are found in the English language today, these etiquettes are not practiced, and oftentimes, the translator falls victim to the confines of literal translation while disregarding the true meanings of the verses as explained by the pious predecessors and the lofty status in the majestic court of Allāh Almighty of those regarding whom the *Qur'ān* speaks of. Many an example can be found of this in the translation of this very verse of the Noble *Qur'ān*.

The Noble *Qur'ān* states:

وَعَصٰۤى اٰدَمُ رَبَّهٗ فَغَوٰى [117]

In translation of this portion of the verse, the renowned translation of Saheeh International reads:

"And Adam disobeyed his Lord and erred."

The translation of Pickthall says:

"And Adam disobeyed his Lord, so went astray."

Yusuf Ali translates this as:

"Thus did Adam disobey his Lord, and allow himself to be seduced."

Such translations which lack the etiquette of the noble courts of Allāh's messengers, upon them be salutations, are also found in translations of the seniors of Deoband. However, it comes as no surprise as this is what is expected from the people who shamelessly insult the Best of Mankind, the Beloved of Allāh, blessings and salutations be upon him.

[117] *Sūrah Ṭā-Hā: 121*

'Abū al-'A`lā Mawdūdī's original Urdu translation has been translated to English as:

"Thus Adam disobeyed his Lord and strayed into error."

Taqī `Uthmānī's Urdu has also been translated to English, and his translation reads:

"And 'Ādam disobeyed his Lord, and erred."

In the presence of a plethora of those who were overwhelmed by the words before them and failed to bear in mind the status of the Noble Prophets, upon them be salutations, Sayyidunā 'Imām 'Aḥmad Riḍā' al-Qādirī, may Allāh have mercy upon him, stands out as someone who accurately displays the meanings of the blessed words while bearing in mind the teachings of the pious predecessors in regard to the caution to be exercised in the court of a Prophet of Allāh, upon him be salutations.

The Noble 'Imām, may Allāh have mercy upon him, translates this portion of the verse as:

اور آدم سے اپنے رب کے حکم میں لغزش واقع ہوئی تو جو مطلب چاہا تھا اس کی راہ نہ پائی

And a [apparent] misstep occurred from 'Ādam in the command of his Lord, so he did not find the route of what he intended. [118]

This is a translation which does not only display exemplary accuracy, but it is one which reflects the creedal matter of believing in infallibility for the Noble Prophets, upon them be

[118] *Kanz al-'Īmān fī Tarjamah al-Qur'ān: Sūrah Ṭā-Hā: 121*

salutations, and the caution one must practice in their courts. May Allāh Almighty reward the 'Imām, may Allāh have mercy upon him, abundantly and allow us to reap the benefits of his services. Moreover, may Allāh Almighty always keep us respectful of all those beloved to Him and allow us to practice exemplary caution when making mention of them.

Just as every Prophet, upon him be salutations, of Allāh Almighty is divinely protected from sin, Sayyidunā 'Ādam, upon him be salutations, is also divinely protected from committing a sin. The occurrence of Sayyidunā 'Ādam, upon him be salutations, eating from this tree was a manifestation of that which had been penned in his book of fate. Allāh Almighty is All-Knowing and had known all along what was to transpire, but Allāh Almighty had honored Sayyidunā 'Ādam, upon him be salutations, by allowing him to meet his fate on Earth alongside receiving the valuable lessons of repentance and witnessing the unrestricted Mercy of Allāh Almighty.

Shaykh 'Ismā`īl Ḥaqqī, may Allāh have mercy upon him, mentions that it was in the divine knowledge of Allāh Almighty that Sayyidunā 'Ādam, upon him be salutations, would surely eat from this tree and thus, he was told to refrain from it so that his eating from the tree becomes a means to an apparent misstep which would ultimately result in repentance, love, and purity.[119]

[119] *Tafsīr Rūḥ al-Bayān, Sūrah al-Baqarah: 35*

Shaykh 'Ismā`īl Ḥaqqī, may Allāh have mercy upon him, then mentions a verse of the Noble *Qur'ān* which relates to this explanation:

إِنَّ اللَّهَ يُحِبُّ التَّوَّابِينَ وَيُحِبُّ الْمُتَطَهِّرِينَ

Indeed, Allāh loves those who repent, and He loves those who are pure.[120]

In conclusion, Sayyidunā 'Ādam, upon him be salutations, was created for the land and *Jannah* was not yet to be his abode forever. Even the *Malā'ikah* were informed of this reality as Allāh Almighty stated:

إِنِّي جَاعِلٌ فِي الْأَرْضِ خَلِيفَةً

I will be creating, in the land, a vice-regent. [121]

Sayyidunā 'Ādam, upon him be salutations, was created to be the *khalīfah* of his Merciful Lord Almighty in the land and in order to fulfill this responsibility, he would have to leave the comforts of Paradise and descend to Earth. This was his fate and destiny.

This is supported by a narration of Sayyidunā 'Abū Hurayrah, Allāh is pleased with him, wherein the Messenger of Allāh, may Allāh send blessings and salutations upon him, describes a debate that transpired between two Prophets of Allāh Almighty, Sayyidunā Mūsā, upon him be salutations, and Sayyidunā 'Ādam, upon him be salutations:

[120] *Sūrah al-Baqarah: 222*

[121] *Sūrah al-Baqarah: 30*

احتج آدم وموسى فقال له موسى أنت آدم الذى أخرجتك خطيئتك من الجنة فقال له آدم
أنت موسى الذى اصطفاك الله برسالاته وبكلامه ثم تلومنى على أمر قدر على قبل أن أخلق
فقال رسول الله صلى الله عليه وسلم فحج آدم موسى مرتين

'Ādam and Mūsā debated so Mūsā said to him, "You are the 'Ādam whose [apparent] misstep caused you to exit Jannah." So, 'Ādam said to him, "You are the Mūsā who Allāh selected for His messenger-hood and His word. Yet, you blame me over an affair which was decreed upon me before I was even created?" Thereafter, the Messenger of Allāh, may Allāh send blessings and salutations upon him, said twice, "Thus, 'Ādam confuted Mūsā." [122]

Sayyidunā 'Ādam's, upon him be salutations, response to Sayyidunā Mūsā's, upon him be salutations, criticism brought him to prefer silence because Sayyidunā Mūsā, upon him be salutations, being the *Kalīm* of Allāh Almighty, recognized the depths of destiny and accepted that this was not a matter in which Sayyidunā 'Ādam, upon him be salutations, could receive blame. This was a matter, alongside his repentance and forgiveness, which was written in his destiny as this would be his path to Earth. None has the right to criticize another for an act which they have sincerely repented for. Sayyidunā Mūsā, upon him be salutations, preferring silence in this regard is proof of this.

[122] *Ṣaḥīḥ al-Bukhārī: 3409*

After having recognized the lofty station of the Noble Prophet 'Ādam, upon him be salutations, and his infallibility, one can see how the events unfolded which became the means for him and his honorable wife, Sayyidatunā Ḥawwā', Allāh is pleased with her, leaving *Jannah*.

While Sayyidunā 'Ādam, upon him be salutations, and Sayyidatunā Ḥawwā', Allāh is pleased with her, resided in *Jannah*, the jealousy in the heart of 'Iblīs for Sayyidunā 'Ādam, upon him be salutations, became amplified and he was constantly on the lookout for a chance to make his attack on them and pull them into his trap of deception. There came a time wherein he eventually saw his chance. Some accounts suggest that he reached *Jannah* himself as even though he was removed from *Jannah*, his access to *Jannah* remained, while according to other reports, he used the creatures of *Jannah* to his benefit against Sayyidunā 'Ādam, upon him be salutations.

Initially, 'Iblīs had attempted to enter *Jannah* but failed in this attempt as he was stopped by the Angels who guarded it. Thereupon, he devised another plan in which he would enter *Jannah* by the aid of a snake he had befriended in Paradise.[123]

In *Jannah*, two creatures, a very beautiful peacock and a snake, would remain in the service of Sayyidunā 'Ādam, upon him be salutations. *Shayṭān* approached the gate of *Jannah* from outside and the peacock had also come to the gate of *Jannah*.

[123] *Tafsīr al-Khāzin, Sūrah al-Baqarah: 36*

The peacock and *Shayṭān* discussed amongst themselves how to bring Sayyidunā 'Ādam, upon him be salutations, and Sayyidatunā Ḥawwā', Allāh is pleased with her, to the gates of Paradise. Thereupon, *Shayṭān* discussed with the snake that it should place him in its mouth and take him to the wall of *Jannah* when Sayyidunā 'Ādam, upon him be salutations, would reach the gate.

After this plot was devised, the peacock began to dance in front of Sayyidunā 'Ādam, upon him be salutations, and Sayyidatunā Ḥawwā', Allāh is pleased with her, attempting to capture their attention. Upon catching their attention, the peacock began to draw back as it continued its dance. As it drew backwards, Sayyidunā 'Adam, upon him be salutations, and Sayyidatunā Ḥawwā', Allāh is pleased with her, advanced towards it, and there came the point that the peacock had eventually reached the gate of *Jannah*. As it danced on and as they followed in its pursuit, they too had arrived at the gate of *Jannah*.

As they approached the gate, the snake sat in wait and as soon as they had reached, the snake took *Shayṭān* in its mouth and came to the wall of *Jannah*.

In this manner, the Noble Sayyidunā 'Ādam, upon him be salutations, encountered the malicious 'Iblīs, and 'Iblīs found his chance to converse with Sayyidunā 'Ādam, upon him be salutations. *Shayṭān* remained outside of *Jannah* while Sayyidunā 'Ādam, upon him be salutations, remained inside, and this conversation transpired.

Regardless of the manner in which the encounter took place, *Shayṭān* had attained his desire of encountering Sayyidunā 'Ādam, upon him be salutations, and thereupon, he said, "I have committed grave blasphemy in your court, I did not prostrate to you, and I have become accursed as a result. Now, I wish to make up for my sin and drive you to such a rank by which you will become pleased with me and the resentment you have for me shall cease." Furthermore, he said, "Do not fall in love with this honor and reverence of yours as, at the end, death is to come to you. All of the amenities and luxuries will come to an end as a result of it."

The Noble Sayyidunā 'Ādam, upon him be salutations, questioned, "What is death?"

The *Shayṭān* fell to the ground and began to demonstrate the state of man at the time wherein he is grasped by the claws of death. He demonstrated the unbearable pain and suffering that man experiences as his soul is removed from his body and upon witnessing such a horrid and dreadful sight, the Noble Sayyidunā 'Ādam, upon him be salutations, and Sayyidatunā Ḥawwā', Allāh is pleased with her, became frightened and asked, "Is there any way to escape this death?"

The Noble *Qur'ān* narrates what *Shayṭān* said to Sayyidunā 'Ādam, upon him be salutations, at this occasion:

فَوَسْوَسَ إِلَيْهِ الشَّيْطٰنُ قَالَ يٰآدَمُ هَلْ أَدُلُّكَ عَلٰى شَجَرَةِ الْخُلْدِ وَمُلْكٍ لَّا يَبْلٰى

The Shayṭān whispered to him, "O 'Ādam, shall I show you the tree of immortality and kingship which does not deteriorate?" [124]

They inquired, "Which tree is it?"

He told them of the tree, and it was the same one from which these honorable people had been prohibited to eat from. They said, "This tree is the means for kingship being taken away. Allāh Almighty has prohibited us from [eating from] this tree. If we eat from this tree, we will fall to His displeasure. Had it been beneficial, why would we have been prohibited to approach it?"

The Holy *Qur'ān* mentions the response of 'Iblīs, he says:

وَقَالَ مَا نَهٰىكُمَا رَبُّكُمَا عَنْ هٰذِهِ الشَّجَرَةِ إِلَّآ أَنْ تَكُوْنَا مَلَكَيْنِ أَوْ تَكُوْنَا مِنَ الْخٰلِدِيْنَ

And he said, "Your Lord only forbade you from this tree lest you two become Angels or of the immortal." [125]

In other words, the wretched 'Iblīs gave deceitful consolations to Sayyidunā 'Ādam, upon him be salutations, telling him that Allāh Almighty had not forbidden him from this tree because it would cause him any harm, but it was due to the responsibilities of the *khalīfah* not being able to be fulfilled by an Angel.

[124] *Sūrah Ṭā-Hā: 120*

[125] *Sūrah al-'A`rāf: 20*

The *khalīfah* would have responsibilities other than the remembrance of Allāh Almighty and the *Malā'ikah* are continually involved solely in worship; the burden of being the *khalīfah* cannot be lifted by an Angel, and by eating from this tree, one becomes an Angel.

Shayṭān further extended his net of deception and said, "Your Lord has not forbidden you from eating from the tree, He has forbidden you from going near it. You do not go near it. I will bring it, and you can eat it then. Moreover, if eating from it is what the Lord prohibited, then the prohibition was at the early time of your creation. At that time, you did not have the ability to digest it, and now, by His grace, you have become strong. Now, eating it will do you no harm."

In summary, he exhausted his efforts trying to persuade Sayyidunā 'Ādam, upon him be salutations, and Sayyidatunā Ḥawwā', Allāh is pleased with her, to eat from the tree, and the wretched *Shayṭān* went to the extent of swearing by Allāh Almighty that he wished well for them and that he was only saying this for their own benefit. These false oaths of his are mentioned in the Noble *Qur'ān*:

وَقَاسَمَهُمَآ إِنِّى لَكُمَا لَمِنَ ٱلنَّـٰصِحِينَ

And he swore to them that, "I, for you both, am a well-wisher." [126]

[126] *Sūrah al-'A`rāf: 21*

Upon such false displays of sincerity, he garnered the trust of Sayyidunā 'Ādam, upon him be salutations. The Noble Sayyidunā 'Ādam, upon him be salutations, did not think that anyone, in all of the creation, would possess the audacity to take false oaths in the majestic name of the Creator Almighty and as a result, Sayyidunā 'Ādam, upon him be salutations, and Sayyidatunā Ḥawwā', Allāh is pleased with her, ate from the tree.[127]

The false oath *Shayṭān* took using the majestic name of Allāh Almighty was one of the leading factors which caused the Noble Sayyidunā 'Ādam, upon him be salutations, to become a victim of *Shayṭān's* treachery. According to a narration of Sayyidunā `Abd Allāh 'ibn `Abbās, Allāh is pleased with them, Allāh Almighty asked the Honorable Sayyidunā 'Ādam, upon him be salutations:

يا آدم ألم يكن فيما أبحتك من الجنة مندوحة عن الشجرة

O Ādam, was there not an alternative for the tree from that I had made permissible for you in Jannah?

Sayyidunā 'Ādam, upon him be salutations, responded:

بلى يا رب وعزتك ولكن ما ظننت أن أحدا يحلف بك كاذبا

Certainly my Lord, by Your honor! However, I did not imagine that anyone would take a false oath by You! [128]

[127] *Details for the incident of leaving Jannah summarized from Tafsīr Na`īmī, Sūrah al-Baqarah: 36*

[128] *Tafsīr al-Khāzin, Sūrah al-Baqarah: 36*

The moment wherein Sayyidunā 'Ādam, upon him be salutations, and Sayyidatunā Ḥawwā', Allāh is pleased with her, became victims of *Shayṭān's* evil doings is mentioned in the Holy *Qur'ān*:

فَاَكَلَا مِنۡهَا فَبَدَتۡ لَهُمَا سَوۡاٰتُهُمَا وَطَفِقَا يَخۡصِفٰنِ عَلَيۡهِمَا مِنۡ وَّرَقِ الۡجَنَّةِ

So, they both ate from it, then their private parts became revealed, and they began fastening over themselves from the leaves of Paradise. [129]

When Sayyidunā 'Ādam, upon him be salutations, and Sayyidatunā Ḥawwā', Allāh is pleased with her, ate from the tree, the heavenly garments worn by the two had been removed from them and this revealed their private areas known as the *`awrah*. The two, exhibiting man's natural disposition to conceal the *`awrah*, rushed to cover their private areas using the leaves of *Jannah*. Up to this point in time, the two had not seen each other's *`awrah* and thus rushed to cover.[130]

This reaction of the Noble Sayyidunā 'Ādam, upon him be salutations, and the Honorable Sayyidatunā Ḥawwā', Allāh is pleased with her, shows that revealing the private areas has always been something which the intellect has despised, and the nature of mankind has detested.[131]

[129] *Sūrah Ṭā-Hā: 121*

[130] *Khazā'in al-`Irfān, Sūrah al-'A`rāf: 20*

[131] *ibid*

The practices of the modern day wherein there is no shame in revealing the private areas or wearing revealing clothing contradict the natural disposition upon which Allāh Almighty has created man, and it is incumbent upon the believing men and women to protect themselves and their children from such blatant displays of shamelessness.

When the two had eaten from the tree, Allāh Almighty commanded for the commencement of life on Earth and said:

وَقُلْنَا اهْبِطُوْا بَعْضُكُمْ لِبَعْضٍ عَدُوٌّ وَلَكُمْ فِي الْأَرْضِ مُسْتَقَرٌّ وَّمَتَاعٌ إِلَى حِيْنٍ

And We said, "Descend! One of you is an enemy to another, and for you, in the land, is residence and provision to a time." [132]

Even while being issued the command to leave *Jannah* for Earth, it can be seen in this verse of the Noble *Qur'ān* that Allāh Almighty continues to manifest His love and mercy towards His Noble and Beloved Prophet Sayyidunā 'Ādam, upon him be salutations. Allāh Almighty gives His Beloved Prophet and the Father of Mankind, upon him be salutations, glad tidings that this residence of his on Earth is "to a time," and eventually, he, being a Noble Prophet of Allāh Almighty, is to return to the abode of the pious and to the luxuries of *Jannah* wherein he shall reside eternally.[133]

[132] *Sūrah al-Baqarah: 36*

[133] *Khazā'in al-`Irfān, Sūrah al-Baqarah: 36*

7

ARRIVING TO EARTH

Acting upon the divine command of Allāh Almighty, the Obedient Sayyidunā 'Ādam, upon him be salutations, and Sayyidatunā Ḥawwā', Allāh is pleased with her, descended to the face of Earth but were sent on Earth to differing locations. Sayyidunā 'Ādam, upon him be salutations, descended from Paradise onto a mountain in a place known as Serendib (*Sarandīb*) in Arabic and described in the books of *Tafsīr* to be in the lands of *Hind*.[134]

The island of Serendib, today, falls in the boundaries of Sri Lanka and the mountain upon which Sayyidunā 'Ādam, upon him be salutations, descended is known as "Adam's Peak" even today.

[134] *Tafsīr al-Khāzin, Sūrah al-Baqarah: 36*

A narration attributed to Sayyidunā `Alī al-Murtaḍā, Allāh is pleased with him, mentions that when Sayyidunā 'Ādam, upon him be salutations, was brought down to Earth, his blessed body was still covered in the leaves from the trees of *Jannah*. As the wind blew, the leaves departed from the blessed body and to whichever tree those leaves reached, it became extraordinarily fragrant. This is the reason that many fragrances such as oud still come from those lands.[135]

When Sayyidunā 'Ādam, upon him be salutations, came down to Earth, he had brought with himself many treasures from *Jannah*. He had brought many types of seeds, three types of fruits, the staff which was to eventually reach the blessed hands of Sayyidunā Mūsā, upon him be salutations, some gold and silver, and some tools for agriculture. At this time, Sayyidunā 'Ādam, upon him be salutations, also had brought the *Ḥajr 'Aswad*. This is the black stone of Paradise which is now placed at a corner of the *Ka`bah*. When this blessed stone was brought from Paradise, its radiance would travel the distance of several miles. Wherever the rays of its radiance reached was deemed the *Ḥaram*.[136]

At this point in time, Sayyidunā 'Ādam, upon him be salutations, was emotionally submerged in the longing for Paradise and of his wife, Sayyidatunā Ḥawwā', Allāh is pleased with her. *Shayṭān* saw this emotional state of his as another opportunity to attack.

[135] *Tafsīr Na`īmī, Sūrah al-Baqarah: 36*

[136] *ibid*

Thus, despite being sent to Earth far away from Sayyidunā 'Ādam, upon him be salutations, he made his way over to him and he grazed his filthy hands over the seeds which Sayyidunā 'Ādam, upon him be salutations, had brought with him. Every seed touched by his filthy hands became poisonous, and every seed the incompetent fool missed preserved its benefit for the children of Sayyidunā 'Ādam, upon him be salutations.[137]

This was a moment of great sorrow and anxiety for Sayyidunā 'Ādam, upon him be salutations, having left Paradise on such terms and being without his wife. Hence, Sayyidunā Jibrīl, upon him be salutations, also made his way down to Earth and called out the blessed words of the *'adhān*. In the duration of the *'adhān*, when Sayyidunā Jibrīl, upon him be salutations, uttered the blessed name of the Master of Creation Sayyidunā Muḥammad al-Muṣṭafā, may Allāh send blessings and salutations upon him, which is the source of peace and tranquility for anyone with a drop of faith in their hearts, Sayyidunā 'Ādam, upon him be salutations, found peace and tranquility, and the anxiety which troubled his heart found its way out.[138]

Although Sayyidunā 'Ādam, upon him be salutations, had found escape from his anxiety, he still faced the profound sorrow of the events which led to him leaving *Jannah*.

137 *ibid*

138 *ibid*

Moreover, his beloved wife, Sayyidatunā Ḥawwā', Allāh is pleased with her, who was a source for his peace, was brought down to the land in Jeddah, a location which caused the distance of seven-hundred parasangs between the only two humans on Earth.[139]

It seems as if the location which Sayyidatunā Ḥawwā', Allāh is pleased with her, was brought down to was called Jeddah in her honor as the word "*jaddah*" means grandmother, and she is the grandmother for all of humankind.

When these two honorable individuals came down to Earth, those who played the role of their enemies were banished from *Jannah* and were each given a punishment of their own.

This snake which used to be in the service of Sayyidunā 'Ādam, upon him be salutations, was an extraordinarily beautiful animal and it had four legs upon which it would walk. However, due to its treachery, the snake was deprived of its legs and was made to travel upon its stomach as a punishment when it was removed from *Jannah*. This snake, when banished from Paradise, landed in the area of *Sijistān* or in Isfahan.[140]

The peacock had also played a role in assisting *Shayṭān*, and it was brought down to Earth in the fields of *Hind*.[141]

[139] *Tafsīr Rūḥ al-Bayān, Sūrah al-Baqarah: 36*

[140] *Tafsīr Na'īmī, Sūrah al-Baqarah: 36*

[141] *Tafsīr Rūḥ al-Bayān, Sūrah al-Baqarah: 36*

Even today, the peacock's beauty is manifest, but due to it being an accomplice in the evil doings of 'Iblīs, its feet were made to become hideous and a contradiction to the rest of its eye-catching build.[142]

'Iblīs, the greatest enemy of all, was exiled from *Jannah* and, this time, his access was permanently revoked. His appearance was made even more unpleasing to the eye and was humiliated to an even greater extent. He was sent down either to a jungle in the proximity of Basra or to the location wherein the wall of Ya'jūj and Ma'jūj currently stands.[143]

In this time on Earth, the Noble Sayyidunā 'Ādam, upon him be salutations, involved himself in the task of farming, and the first task he took upon himself was the knitting of clothing.[144]

142 *Tafsīr Na`īmī, Sūrah al-Baqarah: 36*

143 *ibid*

144 *ibid*

8

THE REPENTANCE

It is the blessed practice of Allāh Almighty that He protects those who are beloved to Him from the evil of wrongdoings. The Noble `Allāmah 'Ismā`īl Ḥaqqī, may Allāh have mercy upon him, presents a narration in this regard:

إذا أحب الله عبدا لم يضره الذنب

When Allāh loves a slave, sin does not harm him.

Shaykh 'Ismā`īl Ḥaqqī, may Allāh have mercy upon him, explains this narration by saying:

أى حفظه من الذنب وإذا وقع فيه وفقه للتوبة والندامة

In other words, He protects him from sin and when he falls into it, He gives him the opportunity for repentance and remorse. [145]

Successfully protecting one's garb from the stain of sin as he carefully treads through the filth which surrounds him is not only something which the intellect perceives to be difficult. Rather, with others diving headfirst into the filth, the likelihood increases of a blemish on the garb resulting from the splashes produced by such divers, and the idea of purity moves further and further away from reach until the intellect deems it impossible.

However, this narration shows that the divine aid of Allāh Almighty can allow one to pass through such filth without a drop touching the clothing. Moreover, if one slips for even a moment, the love of Allāh Almighty gives him the tools to purify himself once again: repentance and remorse. Protection from sin is a result of Allāh's Almighty divine love.

Thus, keeping in mind that Sayyidunā 'Ādam, upon him be salutations, is not an ordinary man, and that he is a beloved Prophet of Allāh Almighty, one can make sense of the emotions exhibited by him even when committing an act which was

[145] *Tafsīr Rūḥ al-Bayān, Sūrah al-Baqarah: 36*

unpreferable (*khilāf al-'awlā*), such an act that if performed by an ordinary man, he would not feel the slightest of remorse or regret. This is an act that is not a sin, it is an act which had a superior alternative. However, when the Infallible Sayyidunā 'Ādam, upon him be salutations, was sent to Earth from *Jannah*, he felt an incredibly profound sense of remorse for what had occurred from him, and this is a manifest display of the degree to which the Noble Prophets, upon them be salutations, of Allāh Almighty are obedient to Him.

The Most Noble and Most Superior Prophet of Allāh Sayyidunā Muḥammad al-Muṣṭafā, may Allāh send blessings and salutations upon him, states:

الندم توبة والتائب كمن لا ذنب له

Remorse is repentance, and the one who repents is like the one who has no sin. [146]

The one who feels remorse for his actions, according to this narration, is like someone who has not even committed the act in the first place. This is the power of remorse on its own and the degree of remorse exhibited by Sayyidunā 'Ādam, upon him be salutations, upon being sent to Earth is surely a sight to see and a lesson for his offspring. The remorse of Sayyidunā 'Ādam, upon him be salutations, was such that it could be read in his behavior and seen in his actions.

[146] *Mishkāh al-Maṣābīḥ: 2363*

His physical state and his behavior are described in the books of exegesis:

إن آدم لما أهبط إلى الأرض مكث ثلاثمائة سنة لا يرفع رأسه

إلى السماء حياء من الله تعالى

Indeed, 'Ādam, when he was sent down to the land, spent three-hundred years without raising his head towards the sky out of the shame of Allāh, the Exalted. [147]

So ashamed of his own actions, Sayyidunā 'Ādam, upon him be salutations, did not dare to look in the direction of the Paradise that was once his abode. He kept his head lowered in humility and awaited the mercy of his Lord Almighty. Sayyidunā 'Ādam, upon him be salutations, and Sayyidatunā Ḥawwā', Allāh is pleased with her, cried to no end as the bounty of *Jannah* slipped from their hands. Sayyidunā `Abd Allāh 'ibn `Abbās, Allāh is pleased with them, says:

بكى آدم وحواء على ما فاتهما من نعيم الجنة مائتى سنة ولم يأكلا

ولم يشربا أربعين يوما

'Ādam and Ḥawwā' cried, upon what slipped away from them of the comfort of Jannah, for two-hundred years and they did not eat or drink for forty days. [148]

[147] *Tafsīr al-Khāzin, Sūrah al-Baqarah: 37*

[148] *ibid*

The oceans of tears shed by Sayyidunā 'Ādam, upon him be salutations, at this time are a testimony to his remorse, and one cannot find such an example throughout all of history of someone shedding tears to attain the pleasure of Allāh Almighty.

The Noble Sayyidunā Dāwūd, upon him be salutations, is well known for the tears which flowed from his eyes, but even those tears of sincerity fall behind when seen in comparison to those of Sayyidunā 'Ādam, upon him be salutations.

لو أن دموع أهل الأرض جمعت لكانت دموع آدم أكثر حيث أصاب الخطيئة لو أن دموع داود
ودموع أهل الأرض جمعت لكانت دموع آدم أكثر حيث أخرجه الله من الجنة

If the tears of all the people of the land are gathered, surely, the tears of 'Ādam would be more when the [apparent] misstep occurred. If the tears of Dāwūd and the tears of the people of the land are gathered, certainly the tears of 'Ādam would be more when Allāh removed him from Jannah.[149]

Another narration details the abundance of tears which flowed from the eyes of Sayyidunā 'Ādam, upon him be salutations.

[149] *ibid*

The Beloved Messenger, may Allāh send blessings and salutations upon him, states:

لو جمع بكاء أهل الدنيا إلى بكاء داود لكان بكاء داود أكثر ولو جمع بكاء أهل الدنيا وبكاء داود إلى بكاء نوح لكان بكاء نوح أكثر ولو جمع بكاء أهل الدنيا وبكاء داود وبكاء نوح عليهما السلام إلى بكاء آدم على خطيئته لكان بكاء آدم أكثر

If the crying of the people of the world is accumulated with the crying of Dāwūd, the crying of Dāwūd would surely be more. If the crying of the people of the world and the crying of Dāwūd is accumulated with the crying of Nūḥ, the crying of Nūḥ would certainly be more. If the crying of the people of the world, the crying of Dāwūd, and the crying of Nūḥ, upon him be salutations, is accumulated with the crying of 'Ādam over his [apparent] misstep, the crying of 'Ādam would certainly be more. [150]

To assist the profound sorrow in the heart and the remorse which flowed from the eyes in the form of tears, Allāh Almighty revealed to Sayyidunā 'Ādam, upon him be salutations, the words to bring to his tongue to find acceptance. Allāh Almighty describes this in the Noble *Qur'ān*:

فَتَلَقّٰۤى اٰدَمُ مِنْ رَّبِّهٖ كَلِمٰتٍ فَتَابَ عَلَيْهِؕ اِنَّهٗ هُوَ التَّوَّابُ الرَّحِيْمُ

Then, 'Ādam learned from his Lord some words so He accepted his repentance. Indeed, it is He who is the Oft-Accepting of Repentance, the Merciful. [151]

[150] *Tafsīr Kabīr, Sūrah al-Baqarah: 37*

[151] *Sūrah al-Baqarah: 37*

The words that were bestowed unto Sayyidunā 'Ādam, upon him be salutations, resulted in his *tawbah*, or repentance, being accepted in the majestic court of Allāh Almighty. What exactly these words were which resulted in achieving the pleasure of Allāh Almighty are a matter of dispute amongst the exegetes of the Noble *Qur'ān*.

One position is that these blessed words of the *tawbah* were:

قَالَا رَبَّنَا ظَلَمْنَا أَنفُسَنَا وَإِن لَّمْ تَغْفِرْ لَنَا وَتَرْحَمْنَا لَنَكُونَنَّ مِنَ الْخَاسِرِينَ

They both said, "O our Lord, we have wronged our own selves, and if You do not forgive us, and have mercy on us, we will surely be from amongst the insufficient." [152]

This is the position which is narrated to be that of Sayyidunā `Abd Allāh 'ibn `Abbās, Allāh is pleased with them, and others.[153]

Another position narrated from 'Imām Mujāhid, may Allāh have mercy upon him, is that these words were:

سبحانك اللهم لا إله إلا أنت ربي ظلمت نفسي فأغفر لي إنك أنت الغفور الرحيم

Glory be to You, O Allāh! There is none worthy of worship except You. My Lord, I have wronged my own self, so forgive me. Indeed, You are the All-Forgiving, the Ever-Merciful. [154]

[152] *Sūrah al-'A`rāf: 23*

[153] *Tafsīr al-Qurṭubī, Sūrah al-Baqarah: 37*

[154] *ibid*

One position says that these words were a conversation that took place between Allāh Almighty and Sayyidunā 'Ādam, upon him be salutations.

Sayyidunā 'Ādam, upon him be salutations, said:

يا رب ألم تخلقني بيدك بلا واسطة

O my Lord, did You not create me with Your power without any medium?

Allāh Almighty responded:

بلى

Of course.

Sayyidunā 'Ādam, upon him be salutations, asked:

يا رب ألم تنفخ في من روحك

O my Lord, did You not inspirit me from a soul of Yours?

Again, Allāh Almighty responded:

بلى

Of course.

Sayyidunā 'Ādam, upon him be salutations, said:

ألم تسكني الجنة

Did You not allow me to sojourn in Paradise?

Allāh Almighty said:

بلى

Of course.

The Noble Sayyidunā 'Ādam, upon him be salutations, said:

يا رب ألم تسبق رحمتك غضبك

O my Lord, does Your mercy not manifest before Your wrath?

Allāh Almighty replied:

بلى

Of course.

Sayyidunā 'Ādam, upon him be salutations, asked:

يا رب إن تبت وأصلحت تردني إلى الجنة

O my Lord, if I repent and make amends, will You return me to Paradise?

Again, Allāh Almighty responded:

بلى

Of course. [155]

[155] *Tafsīr Kabīr, Sūrah al-Baqarah: 37*

In this regard, the Noble Mother of the Believers Sayyidatunā `Ā'ishah al-Ṣiddīqah, Allāh is pleased with her, says:

لما أراد الله أن يتوب على آدم طاف بالبيت سبعا والبيت يومئذ ربوة حمراء فلما صلى ركعتين استقبل البيت وقال اللهم إنك تعلم سرى وعلانيتى فاقبل معذرتى وتعلم حاجتى فأعطنى سؤلى وتعلم ما فى نفسى فاغفر لى ذنوبى اللهم إنى أسئلك إيمانا يباشر قلبى ويقينا صادقا حتى أعلم أنه لن يصيبنى إلا ما كتبت لى وأرضى بما قسمت لى فأوحى الله تعالى إلى آدم يا آدم قد غفرت لك ذنبك ولن يأتينى أحد من ذريتك فيدعونى بهذا الدعاء الذى دعوتنى به إلا غفرت ذنبه وكشفت همومه وغمومه ونزعت الفقر من بين عينيه وجاءته الدنيا وهو لا يريدها

When Allāh intended to accept the repentance of 'Ādam, he circumambulated the House [of Allāh] seven times. The House, in that day, was a red hill.

So, when he prayed two rak`ahs, he faced the House and said, "O Allāh, indeed, You know my private state and my public state, so accept my apology. You know my need, so fulfill my request. You know what is in my heart, so forgive for me my [apparent] misstep. O Allāh, indeed, I ask You for faith that touches my heart and true belief such that I am certain that nothing will ever come to me except what You have written for me and I am pleased with that which You have destined for me."

Then, Allāh, the Exalted, revealed to 'Ādam, "O 'Ādam, I have forgiven, for you, your [apparent] misstep. No one from your offspring will ever come to Me and beseech Me with this supplication that you have besought Me by except that I forgive his sin, remove his sorrows and his agonies, and I take away poverty from his view, and the world comes to him while he has no desire for it." [156]

In this time, the structure of the *Ka`bah* had not yet been constructed, but the location of the *Ka`bah* had always been deemed sacred and the House of Allāh Almighty. There was a red hill in the location of where the *Ka`bah* stands today and thus Sayyidunā 'Ādam, upon him be salutations, performed *ṭawāf* around this red hill.

According to another narration, Sayyidunā 'Ādam, upon him be salutations, and Sayyidatunā Ḥawwā', Allāh is pleased with her, were taught the method of *Ḥajj*, and the words of the repentance were the words which are spoken in the *Ḥajj*. Upon the completion of the *Ḥajj*, they were both given the glad tidings of their forgiveness from the court of Allāh Almighty.[157]

[156] *ibid*

[157] *ibid*

According to another report, these words were Sayyidunā 'Ādam, upon him be salutations, asking Allāh Almighty:

يا رب خطيئتي التي أخطأتها أشيء كتبته علي قبل أن تخلقني أو شيء ابتدعته من قبل نفسي

O my Lord, the [apparent] misstep which I have committed, is it something You have written upon me before You created me or is it something I have initiated on behalf of myself?

Allāh Almighty responded:

بلى شيء كتبته عليك قبل أن أخلقك

Certainly! It is something I have decreed upon you before I created you.

Thereupon, Sayyidunā 'Ādam, upon him be salutations, presented his request:

فكما كتبته علي فاغفره لي

So, just as You have written it upon me, forgive it for me. [158]

Amongst the plethora of narrations detailing the words which resulted in the *tawbah* of Sayyidunā 'Ādam, upon him be salutations, being accepted, one particular position stands out. This is the one which emphasizes the doctrine that this world and all that is within it has been created for the sake of the Master of the Universe Sayyidunā Muḥammad Rasūl Allāh, may Allāh send blessings and salutations upon him.

[158] *Tafsīr al-Ṭabarī, Sūrah al-Baqarah: 37*

This position states that these words that were bestowed unto the Noble Sayyidunā ʻĀdam, upon him be salutations, upon his profound sorrow were the medium (*wasīlah*) of Sayyidunā Rasūl Allāh, may Allāh send blessings and salutations upon him, in the majestic court of Allāh Almighty. Sayyidunā ʻĀdam, upon him be salutations, besought Allāh Almighty for his forgiveness through the *wasīlah* of the Most Superior Creation, may Allāh send blessings and salutations upon him. It was his blessed medium which put an end to an era of sorrow, grief, and remorse. It was for his sake that Allāh Almighty cleansed the slate of Sayyidunā ʻĀdam, upon him be salutations. This is a view recorded by many renowned exegetes of the *Qur'ān* and various scholars of *Ḥadīth*.

ʻImām Qurṭubī, may Allāh have mercy upon him, a renowned *mufassir* of the seventh *hijrī* century, records this position and writes:

رأى مكتوبا على ساق العرش محمد رسول الله فتشفع بذلك فهى الكلمات

He saw written on the pillar of the `Arsh, "Muḥammad is the Messenger of Allāh," so he sought intercession by that. Those were the words [of tawbah]. [159]

In this passage, it is seen that one position regarding the words which were used by Sayyidunā ʻĀdam, upon him be salutations, for his repentance were those he saw written on the `*Arsh* of Allāh Almighty: Muḥammad, may Allāh send blessings and salutations upon him, is the Messenger of Allāh.

[159] *Tafsīr al-Qurṭubī, Sūrah al-Baqarah: 37*

After centuries passed in sorrow, it was the *wasīlah* of Sayyidunā Rasūl Allāh, may Allāh send blessings and salutations upon him, which granted him rescue from his state of remorse.

This position of Sayyidunā Rasūl Allāh, may Allāh send blessings and salutations upon him, being the medium to the acceptance of Sayyidunā 'Ādam's, upon him be salutations, repentance is further supported by `Allāmah Shihāb al-Dīn Sayyid Maḥmūd 'Alūsī, may Allāh have mercy upon him, the thirteenth *hijrī* century author of *Rūḥ al-Ma`ānī*. `Allāmah 'Alūsī, may Allāh have mercy upon him, mentions that Sayyidunā 'Ādam, upon him be salutations, had seen these words inscribed on the *`Arsh* and had presented the blessed personality whose name he had seen written upon it besides the majestic name of Allāh Almighty as a medium in his supplication. Furthermore, he defends the idea that the "*kalimāt* (words)" that were taught to Sayyidunā 'Ādam, upon him be salutations, refer to the blessed entity of Sayyidunā Rasūl Allāh, may Allāh send blessings and salutations upon him, himself.

This, however, causes the objection to come to mind that: how can the word "*kalimāt*" or "words" that were mentioned in this verse of the Holy *Qur'ān* be in reference to a person?

`Allāmah Sayyid 'Alūsī, may Allāh have mercy upon him, responds to this by saying:

وإذا أطلقت الكلمة على عيسى عليه السلام

فلتطلق الكلمات على الروح الأعظم والحبيب الأكرم

When [the word] "kalimah" is applied to `Īsā, upon him be salutations, [the word] "kalimāt" can definitely be applied to the Most Superior Soul and the Most Noble Beloved. [160]

In this passage, `Allāmah 'Alūsī, may Allāh have mercy upon him, reminds the reader that the Noble Sayyidunā `Īsā, upon him be salutations, is referred to as "*Kalimah Allāh,*" or the Word of Allāh Almighty.

This is one of the many titles of Sayyidunā `Īsā, upon him be salutations, and its usage is also seen in the Noble *Qur'ān* as Allāh Almighty says:

إِنَّمَا الْمَسِيحُ عِيسَى ابْنُ مَرْيَمَ رَسُولُ اللَّهِ وَكَلِمَتُهُ أَلْقَاهَا إِلَىٰ مَرْيَمَ وَرُوحٌ مِّنْهُ

The Messiah `Īsā, the son of Maryam, is only a messenger of Allāh and one word of His which He directed towards Maryam, and one soul from Him. [161]

In this verse of the Noble *Qur'ān* the word "*kalimah*" is undoubtedly being used in description of the Noble Sayyidunā `Īsā, upon him be salutations.

[160] *Rūḥ al-Ma`ānī, Sūrah al-Baqarah: 37*

[161] *Sūrah al-Nisā': 171*

Thus, considering this usage, what is the issue if the plural form, "*kalimāt*," is used to describe the Master of all Prophets, peace and blessing be upon him?

'Imām 'Alūsī, may Allāh have mercy upon him, further mentions that even the greatest of Prophets, upon them be salutations, including Sayyidunā `Īsā, upon him be salutations, and Sayyidunā Mūsā, upon him be salutations, are not but a portion from the manifestation of his rays, may Allāh send blessings and salutations upon him, akin to a single flower amidst the vast gardens of his luminosities.[162]

'Imām Ḥākim, may Allāh have mercy upon him, records a narration of Sayyidunā `Umar bin al-Khaṭṭāb, Allāh is pleased with him, detailing this occurrence in which the Messenger of Allāh, may Allāh send blessings and salutations upon him, says:

لما اقترف آدم الخطيئة قال يا رب أسألك بحق محمد لما غفرت لى فقال الله يا آدم وكيف عرفت محمدا ولم أخلقه قال يا رب لأنك لما خلقتنى بيدك ونفخت فى من روحك رفعت رأسى فرأيت على قوائم العرش مكتوبا لا إله إلا الله محمد رسول الله فعلمت أنك لم تضف إلى اسمك إلا أحب الخلق إليك فقال الله صدقت يا آدم إنه لأحب الخلق إلى ادعنى بحقه فقد غفرت لك ولولا محمد ما خلقتك

When 'Ādam committed the [apparent] misstep, he said, "O my Lord, I beseech You, for the sake of Muḥammad, that You forgive me." So, Allāh said, "O 'Ādam, how did you come to know of Muḥammad while I have yet to create him?"

[162] *Rūḥ al-Ma`ānī, Sūrah al-Baqarah: 37*

He said, "O my Lord, because when You created me with Your power, and inspirited me from a soul of Yours, I lifted my head and saw written on the pillars of the `Arsh, 'There is none worthy of worship but Allāh, Muḥammad is the Messenger of Allāh.' Thereupon, I knew that You would not attach to Your name except the most beloved of creation to You." So, Allāh said, "You have spoken the truth O 'Ādam. He is surely the most beloved of creation to Me. Beseech Me for his sake – I have forgiven you. Had it not been for Muḥammad, I would not have created you." [163]

Furthermore, after the mention of this narration, 'Imām Ḥākim, may Allāh have mercy upon him, writes:

هذا حديث صحيح الإسناد

This is a ḥadīth authentic of chain. [164]

Ṭabrānī, in *Mu`jam Ṣaghīr*[165], and Bayhaqī, in *Dalā'il al-Nubūwah*[166], have also recorded similar narrations which are ascribed to Sayyidunā `Umar al-Fārūq, Allāh is pleased with him.

163 *al-Mustadrak `alā al-Ṣaḥīḥayn: 4228*

164 *ibid*

165 *al-Mu`jam al-Ṣaghīr: 992*

166 *Dalā'il al-Nubūwah, Bāb Mā Jā'a fī Taḥadduth Rasūl Allāh, may Allāh send blessings and salutations upon him, bi Ni`mah Rabbihī...*

Moreover, 'Imām Jalāl al-Dīn al-Suyūṭī, may Allāh have mercy upon him, records the narration of 'Ibn al-Mundhir wherein Sayyidunā Jibrīl, upon him be salutations, visits the court of Sayyidunā 'Ādam, upon him be salutations, upon witnessing his profound sorrow and remorse and asks him to say:

إنى أسئلك بجاه محمد عبدك وكرامته عليك أن تغفر لى خطيئتى

Verily, I implore You by the rank of Muḥammad, Your servant, and by his honor in Your court that You forgive, for me, my [apparent] misstep. [167]

By the unfathomable blessings contained within the *wasīlah* of Sayyidunā Rasūl Allāh, may Allāh send blessings and salutations upon him, the seemingly unending centuries of Sayyidunā 'Ādam's, upon him be salutations, remorse had finally come to an end and Sayyidunā 'Ādam, upon him be salutations, had received the glad tidings of his forgiveness from the court of *al-Tawwāb, al-Raḥīm*. How misfortunate are those who view the *wasilāh* of Sayyidunā Rasūl Allāh, may Allāh send blessings and salutations upon him, as an innovation or a form of polytheism while the *mufassirūn* and the *muḥaddithūn* from the scholars of the early periods and the latter periods have mentioned that this was the route towards forgiveness embarked upon by the First Man on Earth, upon him be salutations.

[167] *al-Durr al-Manthūr, Sūrah al-Baqarah: 37*

How unfortunate are those who do not reap the benefits of the key to success mentioned by Allāh Almighty:

يَا أَيُّهَا الَّذِينَ آمَنُوا اتَّقُوا اللَّهَ وَابْتَغُوا إِلَيْهِ الْوَسِيلَةَ وَجَاهِدُوا فِي سَبِيلِهِ لَعَلَّكُمْ تُفْلِحُونَ

O those who have believed, fear Allāh, seek towards Him a medium, and struggle in His way expecting that you find success. [168]

The Noble *Qur'ān* instructs the believers to seek a *wasīlah* to the majestic court of Allāh Almighty, and what *wasīlah* can be more fruitful than of the one He Almighty loves most, peace and blessing be upon him?

Recognizing the lofty rank and status of Sayyidunā Rasūl Allāh, may Allāh send blessings and salutations upon him, he presented his medium in the court of Allāh Almighty, and the fruit of this *wasīlah* was that Allāh forgave him. This *wasīlah* resulted in such an ocean of euphoria in the heart of Sayyidunā 'Ādam, upon him be salutations, that no one has ever experienced.[169] The *Malā'ikah* descended from the sky in droves to attend this celebration, congratulating him, saying:

لتهنك توبة الله يا أبا محمد

Let the forgiveness of Allāh make you happy O 'Abū Muḥammad! [170]

[168] *Sūrah al-Mā'idah: 35*

[169] *al-Durr al-Manthūr, Sūrah al-Baqarah: 37*

[170] *ibid*

Sayyidunā Jibrīl, upon him be salutations, joined these droves and made an announcement addressing the creatures of Earth, "O animals, Allāh has sent His *khalīfah* unto you! Obey him and be obedient to him!"

The sea creatures displayed their obedience by lifting their heads, and the creatures of the land gathered in the court of Sayyidunā 'Ādam, upon him be salutations. Sayyidunā 'Ādam, upon him be salutations, began to pet these animals, and whichever animal his hand reached became domesticated. The animal which was not granted the blessed touch of Sayyidunā 'Ādam, upon him be salutations, remained wild and undomesticated.[171]

Another blessing of this day was that the Arabic language, which had been taken from Sayyidunā 'Ādam, upon him be salutations, upon his exit from *Jannah*, was now restored as his repentance had been accepted. His ability to speak in Arabic had been granted back to him. Until this time on Earth, he would speak in the Syriac (*Suryānī*) language.[172]

Furthermore, upon the acceptance of his repentance, he finally filled the void of loneliness by reuniting with his blessed wife, Sayyidatunā Ḥawwā', Allāh is pleased with her. After having spent centuries apart on Earth, they encountered one another in `*Arafāt* and immediately recognized one another despite the seemingly unending time spent apart.

[171] *Tafsīr Na`īmī, Sūrah al-Baqarah: 37*

[172] *ibid*

This is the reason this location is called *`Arafāt*, as this word denotes a location of recognition.[173]

This day was surely one of immense blessings, and it was one which brought incomparable happiness to Sayyidunā 'Ādam, upon him be salutations. It was on this blessed day of *Jumu`ah* and the sacred day of *`Āshūrā'*, the tenth day of *Muḥarram*, wherein the *tawbah* of Sayyidunā 'Ādam, upon him be salutations, was accepted in the majestic court of Allāh.[174]

This entire occurrence teaches the offspring of Sayyidunā 'Ādam, upon him be salutations, the invaluable lesson of *tawbah* from the mistakes that occur on their behalf. It is very likely that man falls into sin, but this incident teaches man the route to redemption. Sayyidunā Rasūl Allāh, may Allāh send blessings and salutations upon him, states:

كل ابن آدم خطاء وخير الخطائين التوابون

[Nearly] Every son of 'Ādam is a wrongdoer, and the best of the wrongdoers are the repentant. [175]

Sincere *tawbah* gives man a chance to redeem himself and embark on the path of righteousness until death takes him. In today's time, *tawbah*, unfortunately, is seen to be by many as an escape route for the wrongdoings for which they have no intent of abandoning.

[173] *ibid*

[174] *Tafsīr al-Qurṭubī, Sūrah al-Baqarah: 37*

[175] *Jāmi` al-Tirmidhī: 2499*

Many will continue down the path of sin and will occasionally repent just for the sake of giving ease to their conscience. *Tawbah* must be sincere and from the depths of the heart for one's slate to be cleared. Allāh sees past all insincerities. 'Imām Fakhr al-Dīn al-Rāzī, may Allāh have mercy upon him, quoting Ḥujjah al-Islām al-Ghazzālī, may Allāh have mercy upon him, mentions that *tawbah* comes into effect as a result of three chronological affairs: *`ilm*, *ḥāl*, and *`amal*. The first leads to the second, and the second leads to the third.

1. *`Ilm* (knowledge): The first condition of *tawbah* is recognizing the harm of sin and the fact that it is a barrier between man and the divine mercy of Allāh.

2. *Ḥāl* (state): Once an individual acknowledges the harm of sin, he is led to this second condition which is the altering of one's emotional state. Upon recognizing the harm that the sin has caused him, man is faced by a heart that aches over the harms of his action. By knowing he has done wrong, one feels the emotional burden of remorse.

3. *`Amal* (action): Upon receiving the blessing of remorse, one abandons the sin and becomes adamant upon refraining from the sin in the future until their death.[176]

[176] *Tafsīr Kabīr, Sūrah al-Baqarah: 37*

Certainly, *tawbah* is a gift granted to the children of Sayyidunā 'Ādam, upon him be salutations, and a manifestation of the divine mercy of Allāh Almighty.

In a state of worry Sayyidunā 'Ādam, upon him be salutations, said, "O Lord, the offspring are very weak and the deceit of 'Iblīs is very severe. If You do not aid them, then how can they save themselves from 'Iblīs?"

Allāh Almighty responded, "O 'Ādam, your laws were different, and they will have different laws. We will appoint an Angel with every human who will protect him from the whispers of *Shayṭān*. We will keep the door of repentance open for him until the time of his death."

Upon this response from the court of Allāh Almighty, Sayyidunā 'Ādam, upon him be salutations, was relieved and expressed gratitude to Allāh Almighty.[177]

The believer must realize that the doors of *tawbah* are open and must come to this door if he happens to commit a mistake. One must not further himself from the path of guidance upon committing a sin by falling further into the depths of evil. Upon committing a sin, one must acknowledge their wrongdoing and ask for the forgiveness of Allāh Almighty.

[177] *Tafsīr Na'īmī, Sūrah al-Baqarah: 37*

9

THE PROGENY

The Noble Parents of Mankind, Sayyidunā 'Ādam, upon him be salutations, and Sayyidatunā Ḥawwā', Allāh is pleased with her, were the only people on the face of the Earth, and it was up to them to populate these uninhabited lands. Together, Sayyidunā 'Ādam, upon him be salutations, and Sayyidatunā Ḥawwā', Allāh is pleased with her, had a total of forty-one children. Forty of their children were the result of twenty pregnancies. [178] The children of Sayyidunā 'Ādam, upon him be salutations, and Sayyidatunā Ḥawwā', Allāh is pleased with her, would be born in pairs as fraternal twins of whom one would be a male and one would be a female.[179]

[178] *al-'Anwār al-Muḥammadīyah, al-Maqṣad al-'Awwal*

[179] *Khazā'in al-`Irfān, Sūrah al-Mā'idah: 27*

In this time, the law of *nikāḥ* and procreation was that a man would not marry the woman who was born as his twin. He would marry a woman born as a result of another pregnancy. In this time, wherein the dwellers of the Earth were limited to the progeny of Sayyidunā 'Ādam, upon him be salutations, there was no other way for procreation.[180]

From the first of these pregnancies, Qābīl and his twin sister 'Iqlīmā were born, and after one year, from another pregnancy, Hābīl and his sister Layūdā were born.[181]

Sayyidunā 'Ādam, upon him be salutations, had intended to fix the marriage of Qābīl with Layūdā, and that of Hābīl with 'Iqlīmā. However, the elder brother, Qābīl, protested this will of his noble father, upon him be salutations, and insisted on marrying his own twin sister, 'Iqlīmā, due to her being more attractive.[182]

Upon his protesting, Sayyidunā 'Ādam, upon him be salutations, attempted to reason with Qābīl saying, "She was born with you and is hence your sister. Your marriage to her is not permissible."

In response to this sincere advice of his noble father, upon him be salutations, Qābīl adapted a tone of disrespect and responded, "This is your opinion, not the command of Allāh."

[180] *ibid*

[181] *Tafsīr Na`īmī, Sūrah al-Mā'idah: 27*

[182] *Khazā'in al-`Irfān, Sūrah al-Mā'idah: 27*

After his attempt of reasoning with Qābīl, Sayyidunā 'Ādam, upon him be salutations, said, "Both of you bring a sacrifice. Whoever's sacrifice is accepted is deserving of 'Iqlīmā."[183]

This occurrence is mentioned in the Noble *Qur'ān*:

وَاتْلُ عَلَيْهِمْ نَبَاَ ابْنَيْ اٰدَمَ بِالْحَقِّ اِذْ قَرَّبَا قُرْبَانًا فَتُقُبِّلَ مِنْ اَحَدِهِمَا وَلَمْ يُتَقَبَّلْ مِنَ الْاٰخَرِ
قَالَ لَاَقْتُلَنَّكَ قَالَ اِنَّمَا يَتَقَبَّلُ اللّٰهُ مِنَ الْمُتَّقِيْنَ

And recite to them the true report of 'Ādam's two sons. When each of the two offered a sacrifice, then it was accepted from one of them, and it was not accepted from the other. He said, "I swear, I will murder you." He said, "Allāh only accepts from the pious." [184]

Upon being instructed by their father, upon him be salutations, to present individual sacrifices in the court of Allāh Almighty, Qābīl, who was a farmer, presented a lousy heap of wheat, and Hābīl, who would tend to animals, brought forth a very pleasing sheep as his sacrifice. Qābīl had consumed the good wheat that he had in his possession by himself and presented, in the majestic court of Allāh Almighty, that which was unpresentable to begin with.[185]

At the time of presenting their individual sacrifices, the intent in the heart of Qābīl was that even if his sacrifice is not accepted, he would not cease the pursuit for 'Iqlīmā.

[183] *ibid*

[184] *Sūrah al-Mā'idah: 27*

[185] *Tafsīr Na`īmī, Sūrah al-Mā'idah: 27*

Hābīl, on the other hand, had brought his sacrifice with utmost sincerity. He thought, "I am pleased with the command of Allāh. I accept whatever decision is made."[186]

In that day and age, a fire would come from the sky and snatch the sacrifice which was accepted in the court of Allāh Almighty and the people would learn of the acceptance, or lack thereof, immediately. Thus, a fire came from the sky and snatched the sacrifice of Hābīl leaving the wheat of Qābīl behind. This caused Qābīl to become enraged with a fire of malice and jealousy in his heart.[187] This fire grew to the point wherein he could not contain it, and he had never tried his hand at extinguishing this fire. He allowed the flames of this fire in his heart to rise until it made way to his tongue and eventually to his actions.

When Sayyidunā 'Ādam, upon him be salutations, had departed to Makkah Mukarramah for *Ḥajj*, Qābīl found his chance in the lack of his father's supervision and said to Hābīl, "I swear I will murder you!"

Hābīl inquired, "Why?!"

Qābīl responded, "Because your sacrifice was accepted and not mine, and you have become deserving of 'Iqlīmā! There is dishonor for me in this!"[188]

[186] *ibid*

[187] *Khazā'in al-`Irfān, Sūrah al-Mā'idah: 27*

[188] *ibid*

Upon these threats from his brother, Hābīl informed him, "Allāh only accepts from the pious."

He reminded his brother that he is not at fault for his sacrifice not being accepted. It was the result of his own doings. Had he been one to fear Allāh Almighty, his sacrifice would have been accepted.[189] However, he chose to disrespect their father and go against him. The fear of Allāh Almighty would not have allowed him to speak to their father as he had spoken, and it would not have allowed him to pursue that which was lawfully not to be his.

The mention of this encounter continues in the Noble *Qur'ān*:

لَئِنۢ بَسَطتَ إِلَيَّ يَدَكَ لِتَقۡتُلَنِي مَآ أَنَا۠ بِبَاسِطٖ يَدِيَ إِلَيۡكَ لِأَقۡتُلَكَۖ إِنِّيٓ أَخَافُ ٱللَّهَ رَبَّ ٱلۡعَٰلَمِينَ

"Surely, if you extend your hand towards me to kill me, I will not extend my hand to you to kill you. I fear Allāh, the Lord of the Worlds."[190]

Hābīl told Qābīl that he would not try to kill him even if Qābīl were to attempt to murder him. The fear of Allāh Almighty in his heart would prevent him from committing such a horrid act despite being physically stronger than Qābīl.[191]

189 *ibid*

190 *Sūrah al-Mā'idah: 28*

191 *Khazā'in al-`Irfān, Sūrah al-Mā'idah: 28*

The mention of the incident continues:

اِنِّیۤ اُرِیۡدُ اَنۡ تَبُوۡٓاَ بِاِثۡمِیۡ وَ اِثۡمِكَ فَتَكُوۡنَ مِنۡ اَصۡحٰبِ النَّارِ وَ ذٰلِكَ جَزٰٓؤُا الظّٰلِمِیۡنَ

"Indeed, I intend that you bear my sin and your sin, and thus you become of the companions of the fire. That is the punishment of the unjust." [192]

The Noble *Qur'ān* further reports the occurrence:

فَطَوَّعَتۡ لَهٗ نَفۡسُهٗ قَتۡلَ اَخِیۡهِ فَقَتَلَهٗ فَاَصۡبَحَ مِنَ الۡخٰسِرِیۡنَ

Thus, his ego incited him to the murder of his brother, so he killed him, and became of the deprived. [193]

Qābīl had committed the first murder on Earth. Moreover, this was not only the first murder on Earth, but it was also the first death of any human.

Thus, he was in a state of confusion as to what he shall do with the body of his brother and carried the corpse on his back for some time. [194]

[192] *Sūrah al-Mā'idah: 29*

[193] *Sūrah al-Mā'idah: 30*

[194] *Khazā'in al-'Irfān, Sūrah al-Mā'idah: 30*

Thereupon, Allāh Almighty showed him the procedure of how to deal with a corpse:

فَبَعَثَ اللّٰهُ غُرَابًا يَّبْحَثُ فِي الْاَرْضِ لِيُرِيَهٗ كَيْفَ يُوَارِيْ سَوْءَةَ اَخِيْهِ قَالَ يٰوَيْلَتٰۤى اَعَجَزْتُ اَنْ
اَكُوْنَ مِثْلَ هٰذَا الْغُرَابِ فَاُوَارِيَ سَوْءَةَ اَخِيْ فَاَصْبَحَ مِنَ النّٰدِمِيْنَ

So Allāh sent a crow scratching at the ground to show him how to hide the corpse of his brother. He said "Woe to me! I could not even be like this crow that I would hide the corpse of my brother." Thus, he became of the remorseful. [195]

It is narrated that two crows began to fight amongst one another, and one killed the other. The surviving crow began to dig the Earth with its beak and placed the dead crow into the ground. Thereafter, it covered the dead crow in dirt. Witnessing this, Qābīl learned that the corpse of his brother should be buried in the ground, and he acted accordingly by digging up the Earth and burying his brother therein.[196]

The incident which took place amongst the earliest of humankind serves as a lesson for the humans even today. Man should surrender their wills and desires into the court of Allāh Almighty and submit to His divine command. Upon sacrificing one's own desires to obey the command of Allāh Almighty, one is safeguarded from a remorse that eats away at the heart as he grows to become wiser.

[195] *Sūrah al-Mā'idah: 31*

[196] *Khazā'in al-`Irfān, Sūrah al-Mā'idah: 31*

One must know that the command of Allāh Almighty is better for him, whether he understands it or not. Had Qābīl submitted to the will of Allāh Almighty, he would not have faced the immense degree of embarrassment that he experienced as he challenged his noble father, upon him be salutations. Furthermore, instead of being jealous of the bounties granted to others, one should direct their attention to the bounties they themselves have received and involve their hearts and tongues in displays of gratitude to Allāh Almighty.

At this point, one of Sayyidunā 'Ādam's, upon him be salutations, children had departed from the domain of Earthly life. There were now thirty-nine of the forty children who were born in pairs to be married off to one another. However, filling the void of oddity and the lack of a spouse for one of the twenty women, the Noble Prophet of Allāh, Sayyidunā Shīth, upon him be salutations, was born without a twin.[197]

Sayyidunā Shīth, upon him be salutations, was the son from the progeny of Sayyidunā 'Ādam, upon him be salutations, who was bestowed the crown of prophethood following in the blessed footsteps of his father. It was this honorable son of his who was given the honor to carry the *nūr* (light) of the Seal of Prophethood Sayyidunā Muḥammad, may Allāh send blessings and salutations upon him. This was a light that was kept within the being of Sayyidunā 'Ādam, upon him be salutations.

[197] *Tafsīr Na`īmī, Sūrah al-Mā'idah: 27*

He transferred this light to his blessed wife, and she birthed the next carrier of this blessed light, Sayyidunā Shīth, upon him be salutations. This is the reason that, of a total of forty-one children, Sayyidunā Shīth, upon him be salutations, was born alone; the carrier of this blessed light is matchless and was thus born without a match. This was in honor of the light which he was to carry.[198]

Sayyidunā 'Ādam, upon him be salutations, related his bequest to Sayyidunā Shīth, upon him be salutations, that this pure light shall only be transferred to pure carriers. He shall marry a pure woman to carry this light after him and hand this light down to the next generation. Sayyidunā Shīth, upon him be salutations, related this bequest to his son, and every carrier of this blessed light related the same to the next carrier amongst their offspring.[199] Thus, this light went from pure men to pure women, generation after generation, until this light was birthed by Sayyidah 'Āminah, Allāh is pleased with her.

[198] *al-'Anwār al-Muḥammadīyah, al-Maqṣad al-'Awwal*

[199] *ibid*

10

THE LEGACY

Eventually came a time wherein Sayyidunā 'Ādam, upon him be salutations, would veil himself from the gaze of the world and would set off to the realm of the afterlife.

When the time came near wherein Sayyidunā 'Ādam, upon him be salutations, would sample the taste of death, he became very reserved and would not speak except a little. He would remain involved exclusively in the *dhikr* (remembrance) of Allāh Almighty.[200]

As his final moments of Earthly life approached, he felt the desire to consume the fruits of Paradise. He commanded his sons to go to the *Ka`bah* and beseech Allāh that He fulfill his wish.

[200] *Tafsīr Na`īmī, Sūrah al-Baqarah: 37*

Upon receiving this command, the sons set off to the *Ka`bah*. As they reached, they were met by the likes of Sayyidunā Jibrīl, upon him be salutations, and other *Malā'ikah*. Thereupon, the sons conveyed the wish of their father to the *Malā'ikah*, and the *Malā'ikah* said, "Come with us. We have brought the fruits of *Jannah* with ourselves."

Thereafter, they all came to the court of Sayyidunā 'Ādam, upon him be salutations. Upon seeing the *Malā'ikah*, Sayyidatunā Ḥawwā', Allāh is pleased with her, began to feel fear and wished to hide herself in the clothing of Sayyidunā 'Ādam, upon him be salutations. Sayyidunā 'Ādam, upon him be salutations, thus said, "Ḥawwā', move away from me. Do not be a barrier between myself and the delegates of my Lord."

The pure soul of Sayyidunā 'Ādam, upon him be salutations, was taken from his blessed body by the *Malā'ikah* and they said, "The method by which we shroud and bury your father, you should do the same."

Sayyidunā Jibrīl, upon him be salutations, had brought a sheet, fragrance, and sidr leaves from *Jannah*. Using these bounties of *Jannah*, Sayyidunā Jibrīl, upon him be salutations, bathed him, applied fragrance to him, and shrouded him. The *Malā'ikah* carried the blessed body to the *Ka`bah* and prayed the *ṣalāh* of *janāzah* over him which was led by Sayyidunā Jibrīl, upon him be salutations.

In one narration, the body of Sayyidunā 'Ādam, upon him be salutations, was carried by one-hundred-fifty men of his progeny.

Thereafter, Sayyidunā 'Ādam, upon him be salutations, was brought to *Minā*, at a location close to *Masjid Khayf*, and was buried at this location.[201]

Upon the passing of Sayyidunā 'Ādam, upon him be salutations, the population of the world had reached forty thousand, and these were all his own children, grandchildren, or great-grandchildren.[202]

Sayyidatunā Ḥawwā', Allāh is pleased with her, joined her blessed spouse in the life which proceeds life and was laid to rest in the city of Jeddah.[203]

When the time of her passing approached, one hundred thousand of her offspring had scattered across the land.[204]

Sayyidunā 'Ādam, upon him be salutations, and Sayyidatunā Ḥawwā', Allāh is pleased with her, are the father and mother to all of mankind and they left behind a legacy of lessons within their stories that should be a means of guidance for their progeny.

[201] *Tafsīr Na`īmī, Sūrah al-Baqarah: 36*
[202] *Tafsīr Na`īmī, Sūrah al-Baqarah: 37*
[203] *Tafsīr Na`īmī, Sūrah al-Baqarah: 36*
[204] *Tafsīr Na`īmī, Sūrah al-Nisā': 1*

May Allāh Almighty accept this work, forgive any shortcomings, and grant their offspring the opportunity to adhere to the path of he who is the Master of all Mankind, may Allāh send blessings and salutations upon him. *'Āmīn*!

تمت بحمد الله

ABOUT THE AUTHOR

Muftī Sayyid `Abdul Ṣamad al-Qādirī is a *murīd* (spiritual disciple) of Sayyidī Tāj al-Sharī`ah Muftī 'Akhtar Riḍā Khān and a dedicated student of Muftī Faizān ul-Muṣṭafā al-Qādirī, the esteemed grandson of Ṣadr al-Sharī`ah. He graduated as a Muftī in Madīnah Munawwarah at the hands of his teacher in Ramaḍān 1444 AH. He has been granted *khilāfah* by the son of Tāj al-Sharī`ah, Qā'id al-Millah Muftī `Asjad Riḍā' Khān and many *'ijāzāt* by Muḥaddith Kabīr `Allāmah Ḍiyā' al-Muṣṭafā al-Qādirī. He is scholar trusted by the likes of Muftī Zāhid Ḥussain al-Qādirī and Muftī 'Afthāb Cāssim. Notably, Muftī `Abdul Ṣamad serves as the lead author and translator for TheSunniWay, a significant initiative led by Muftī Zāhid Ḥussain al-Qādirī, through which this book is presented. Currently, he resides in Silver Spring, Maryland, USA.

TheSunniWay

www.ingramcontent.com/pod-product-compliance
Lightning Source LLC
Chambersburg PA
CBHW021641120626
46545CB00002B/650
* 9 7 8 1 9 5 7 7 7 3 3 8 4 *